TRAVEL THERAPY

Changing Lives
One Trip at a Time

Stacy Kim Johnston, Ph.D.

(Psychologist, Singer/Songwriter, World Traveler, and Retreat Host)

DISCLOSURE STATEMENT

This book contains advice and information related to mental and behavioral health as well as travel. In terms of psychological advice, it is not intended to replace any services you may be receiving from your regular provider, but can be used to supplement any current treatment. All efforts have been made to ensure accuracy of the information contained in this book as of the date of publication. The publisher and author disclaim liability for any medical or psychological outcomes that may occur as a result of applying suggestions in this book. All persons mentioned in this book have given permission to have their stories and statements published.

ISBN: 979-8-218-24010-3 (paperback)
ISBN: 979-8-218-24471-2 (hardcover)
ISBN: 979-8-218-24064-6 (e-book)

THE PURPOSE OF THIS BOOK

What you are about to read is not just a "Self-Help" book, nor is it just a "Travel Guide". I have uniquely combined both ideas and explain how they enhance one another. Traveling the world continues to change my life and I am inspired by bringing people together to experience and find joy in creating more meaningful connections shared both near and far.

Although I will take you to many countries throughout this book, wandering within yourself with a "traveling mind" (whether it be in actuality or theoretically) will also keep you from being stagnant. A traveling mind will allow you to feel engaged in life no matter where you are. I try to be open and free myself of judgement as I go through life. When I write, I therefore allow my stream of consciousness to be accessible to others. My hope is that you, the reader, will enjoy going on this journey with me and develop a *traveling mind* as well.

For those who have not traveled much or at all, this book is designed to inspire you to see the world. However, I realize many do not want or cannot physically go to the amazing places that will be mentioned. This book is written in such a way that it can still benefit you by allowing expansion right where you are by helping you explore parts of yourself not previously apparent. This can also lead to enhancement in relationships you already have, or will have in the future. For those who love travel and are eager for your next trip, I offer transformational journeys (yes *literally* taking you with me!) to actually experience places together beyond the pages in this book.

For now, I hope you enjoy my travel stories to learn from, my itineraries to inspire you, and my psychological essays with writing exercises to help you self-reflect. Whatever your curiosity is, make the unknown known and keep growing while you can, wherever you can.

TABLE OF CONTENTS

GENERAL ACKNOWLEDGEMENTS

I would like to first thank my wonderful friends and family who believe in me, support my writing this book, have shown interest in my group travel trips, and are willing to share the greatest gift you can give a person, which is your time. I want to therefore thank anyone who is reading this right now because you could be doing anything else in this moment, but are instead choosing to pick up this book to decide if it is a good fit for you. Thank you for being curious. More personal acknowledgments can be found at the end of this book.

SECTION I
MY STORY

CHAPTER 1

WHAT DRIVES ME

Being Human First

The first half of my life was not centered around traveling the world, healing others, or writing books, but rather building my character. We are not born knowing what we know as adults, nor are we expected to. We need to learn from our mistakes, heal ourselves before healing others, and always remember that our imperfections do not define us. We should embrace all of our parts, for better and for worse. I try to remind people when they make the comment, "You should know that, being a psychologist", that I am human first and a psychologist second. I am a human being before my role as a mother, daughter, wife, or friend. You must give yourself permission to make mistakes. Please do not carry the burden of the world on your shoulders just because others expect that of you. If they do, they too, need the reminder.

We all have strengths and weaknesses. In our weakest moments, we need to remember how to overcome challenges and that we are capable of incredible and unfathomable things. Being human is a frustration at times, but simultaneously the most amazing thing to be. Being human is real and being real is human. When you learn to forgive yourself, even if others don't, their unrealistic expectations become obvious to you. When people forget about the "human factor" and try to be the perfectionist everyone wants them to be, they end up losing themselves. I, of course, went through phases where I didn't know myself and had to re-invent myself countless times.

I've had my share of mistakes when younger. I was a tomboy and, being in touch with my masculine side, was a stubborn, very independent, rebellious trouble maker. I even lied at times to get my way. As a young teen, I became in touch with my feminine side, got into make-up, attracting men, and in desperation to be liked, adopted people -pleasing behaviors. This led me to being more or less a "shell" of a person (and regretfully have been described by others as such) simply because I didn't actually know who I was, or perhaps it was that I had "lost" myself.

In my young adulthood I was raising two wonderful children, Rachel and Josh, who are now grown adults. I did my best to raise them with what I knew back then, but had a difficult divorce while transitioning from parenting as a couple to "half-time" as a single parent. In my experience, the reality of being "half time" did not "feel" that way when your heart is with your children 100% of the time. I was there for them, but I, of course, have some regrets about things I could have done better. Once you have wisdom it gets much easier, but that only comes with life experience, so the benefits sometimes come after the fact.

This lesson also played out in my adult relationships. Through losing my first boyfriend of four years in a motorcycle accident, being married then divorced after eleven years, to dating men that were not in my best interest for a number of years, taught me many lessons. Thankfully, I found myself and later also found my partner, Jeff (who you will be hearing much more about), to share my life with.

Through years of experience and growth from my psychological studies, life responsibilities, and relationship experiences, I came to know who I am. Now I accept myself as a whole person — the wonderful qualities as well as the limitations and am always working to improve. The healer I am today would not exist without going through those phases, so I am grateful for them. Even through tragedy, we gain.

Being a Psychologist

Becoming a licensed psychologist and running your own practice takes many years to establish. You have to account for the ten years of schooling/internship/licensure requirements, then add the years it takes to build a reputation and establish a consistent flow of clients. Although this meant sacrificing other interests and putting things (such as traveling) on hold, I would not have traded it for the *world* (no pun intended).

I started my journey as a psychologist just being curious about people at a young age. My father taught me that there is no such thing as a stupid question and that the smartest people are the ones who are curious because they ask the most questions. Luckily, I was never a shy person so did not have difficulty in this regard. Coupled with my openness to talk about anything and everything, I became an easy person for people to confide in.

In high school, my girlfriends called me Dr. Ruth because I was never embarrassed to discuss personal issues and, although I am not sure I had all the answers about sex at the ripe age of fifteen, I shared whatever I knew and my friends felt better after our discussions. It may have been more about what they were able to express to me versus any real knowledge I could offer them at that time. In retrospect, I think what really started to blossom at that time in my life was my empathy for others. Fortunately, this compassion came naturally. I simply cared and made time to listen.

Now that I am in my mid 50's and I have some life experience and wisdom to offer, I'm more than just an empathic ear. Since I had the foundation at a young age to be in the helping profession, I never regretted my career choice in becoming a licensed psychologist as an adult because it always felt like home to me. I have a passion for guiding people to reach their full potential. My philosophy is to not pathologize weaknesses, but rather maximize strengths. When a person cannot see their strengths, I do my best to make them salient by being a good listener and mirroring back what they do not see in themselves.

My experiences have ranged from in-home services with developmentally disabled, an inner-city crisis clinic, inpatient hospital setting, college campus counseling center, and my private practice, where I spent most of my professional years. I have serviced various ages from children to elders. I have worked with diverse psychological challenges; the common anxiety/depression combo (sometimes it is just one or the other, but often it comes as a pair), PTSD (not just with war Vets but also victims of sexual and physical abuse), Bipolar Disorder, Obsessive-Compulsive Disorder, Substance Abuse and other addictive behaviors (such as gambling, pornography, and sex addiction), anger management, couples counseling and marital issues including divorce mediation, and other dyad situations such as mother-daughter/ father-son issues, and bereavement. I have chosen to stay varied in my focus as to avoid the common "burn-out" that many psychologists face.

In my 30 years of professional service, only a few cases have been referred out, knowing my limits and acknowledging I simply cannot help everyone. My practice has involved individual therapy, family therapy, as well as group therapy. I co-led an anger management group for court-ordered men as well as a non-mandated men's group, and currently have had the privilege of running a women's group with my daughter for over a year now. Group dynamics are interesting and often times increase cohesion and bonding in ways that individual therapy cannot. No one likes to feel like they're alone in the world and they never really are. Groups give reassurance which is why I enjoy leading them.

Being a Group Leader

Besides my work as a psychologist, I have always been a social person and exhibit the ability to make friends quickly, and not just the kind of friendships that fade with the sun at the end of the day. I have been fortunate enough to have countless lifelong friendships and I know what it takes to sustain these relationships. I have either naturally adopted or been given the role of group leader in different situations. I think it comes naturally for me because I thoroughly enjoy planning events and get togethers more than most.

In retrospect, college is when my confidence really blossomed. I can clearly see the difference between my younger self and my current self. In my earlier years, I was more of a follower, someone who wanted to fit in and be liked. Therefore, I did not always speak up for myself or even have an opinion at all for fear it would not be listened to, or even worse, shot down. Once my high school group of friends went their separate ways after graduation however, I seemed to become the glue that kept this circle together. When I was away at college, I became the initiator and planner for our reunions whenever I returned "home" to visit. It was rare that my friends would see each other if it weren't for my organizing a get-together.

I was told by these friends that they appreciated my efforts because, without me, they may have lost contact all together. I didn't feel it was much effort at all, just something I wanted to do. It was natural for me to plan get-togethers, and more importantly, to follow through with those plans. To me maintenance of life-long friendships felt like a little effort with a huge reward.

In later years and in my professional life, I have become the retreat planner for the group practice, Southern California Psychology Centers (SCPC), I belong to. Although most of us work remotely now, due the pandemic, and do not see each other on a daily basis, at least once a year I am asked to plan a weekend experience to bring us all together in a meaningful way. The CEO of SCPC and past president of the San Diego Psychological Association (SDPA), Dr. Saurabh Gupta, nominated me to be Chair of the Events Committee. I was honored to accept and served in that position for two years. What I like most is creating an environment for people to connect and find common ground with one another. I have been able to implement this concept in different therapy groups that I've run over the years.

My goal is always to bring people together in a way that keeps them present and unified. Our clearest and fondest memories are from times when we were most present and connected. When I have had opportunities to plan events, people later told me how memorable they were and asked when the next one will be. That is incredibly satisfying and motivates me to build that momentum to bigger events, such as leading group travel retreats throughout the world.

In addition to the self-awareness that group therapy and daily/weekend workshops provide, there is an entirely new element when you travel outside your familiar environment. Having distance from routines, responsibilities, and expectations allows room for deeper self-discovery.

CHAPTER 2

INSPIRING PEOPLE IN MY LIFE WHO HAVE UNIQUE STORIES ABOUT TRAVELING

I want to introduce you to some of the people that have inspired me with their stories and travel adventures. Each has added so much wisdom and insight into the world of travel.

Let me start first with Anthony Bourdain, whom I never had the opportunity to interview for this book, but felt it appropriate to say a few words here regarding his contributions to the travel world. Although he focused mainly on food, he had a way of connecting with locals and making friends all over the world with his television series, Anthony Bourdain: Parts Unknown. It was not just the high end, fancy restaurants that he took us to. Instead, he exhibited passion for digging deep into history, food culture, and the souls of each destination. You often saw him sitting on a plastic chair in a rugged part of town, swatting flies away from his food as he conversed with locals. It was unfortunate Bourdain's mental health issues were not addressed. From the outside, no-one would have guessed that someone with seemingly such a perfect life would choose to end it. As a psychologist, I wonder when and what type of intervention could have saved his beautiful soul. Despite the fact that Anthony is no longer with us, his fame was well-deserved as he left us with great contributions to the world of travel. He led by example with his openness to food and people, bravery in the unfamiliar, and appreciation of all walks of life in his remarkable journeys.

Although the following interviewees may not be as well-known as Anthony Bourdain, their influence on what motivates me to look within myself has helped tremendously and I appreciate them for being a part of my life.

Brittany Bamrick is a marvelous yoga teacher and one of the leaders for **Bliss Camp Yoga Retreats**. I met her on a week-long trip I attended with my daughter in Tulum, Mexico. From the minute we arrived at the beautiful resort, we were in good hands and well-taken care of with Brittany's warm and welcoming presence. She lived and breathed what she taught everyone and her genuineness gained my trust and utmost respect as a group leader. She also worked well with her cofounder and yoga teacher Ashley, who also has a big heart.

I was incredibly inspired by how they handled all details of the week. They were not just available, but interacted in a deep and meaningful way with 30 travelers on the trip. They made everyone feel like family, with many repeat travel yogis. Brittany has a two year-old daughter whom she brought along and it was amazing to see how confident this little girl was and how she thrived in such a loving, accepting environment that Brittany creates. In addition, she is learning to love travel at a young age. Although I did not know Brittany or Ashley before that week of "Bliss", and the name is really fitting, their magical environment had such a huge impact on me which turned my life in a new direction. It was that week that actually prompted me to write this book, as will be further explained in Chapter Six. In that chapter I will also provide the contact information for those interested in learning more about Bliss Camp Yoga Retreats.

I live in a high rise building in downtown San Diego and one of the best things about our building is that it provides a sense of community. The people really do care about each other in this building of 39 floors and over 200 units. We have happy hours once a month, holiday parties, and as of late, I've had a few singing performances as well. It is a very welcoming community and I cherish the friends we have made here. I was fortunate to interview a few neighbors for their significant insight, unique stories, and savvy approach to traveling.

Debbi and Mike L. are probably the most widely and varied travelers I have ever met having traveled to over 90 countries across the globe. They are very hard working individuals – Debbi being an OBGYN and Mike owning a cabinet and home improvement company. By the time their two children had completed high school, each had already traveled to 50 countries! Their reason for offering them this opportunity at such a young age was to teach them the importance of understanding and appreciating people from different cultures. What a beautiful gift to pass onto their children and now they too have the travel bug for life. Debbi and Mike are not waiting until retirement to explore the world, but are doing it while physically able, and I wholeheartedly agree with that concept.

Debbi has not only traveled for pleasure, but also has done incredible missionary work in poverty-stricken areas around the globe with her medical background. Typically, Mike does not accompany Debbi on the trips that involve helping women with medical and birthing crises. However, on one mission he contributed his cabinetry skills and build a structure for a community she was working with.

Debbi fulfilled one of her bucket list goals of flying all the way around the world! The only feasible way to do it was to purchase several one-way flights and fly from San Diego to Tokyo, Tokyo to Hanoi, Hanoi to Singapore, and Singapore to Amsterdam. Once in Amsterdam, she traveled to Bucharest, Romania and took trains to different cities ending in Budapest, Hungary circling back to Amsterdam. From there, she finally flew back home. For the most part she was comfortable in her business class seats, but one night she had to sleep on plastic chairs all night at a rather secluded airport in Vietnam, which was not the plan.

Debbi's story reminded me of a crazy travel plan of Jeff's where he found a flash deal on one of the airlines from LA to Singapore at $500 RT that he didn't want to pass up. He asked me if I wanted to go for a 3 day weekend. What we didn't plan for was that our direct flight from LAX to Singapore was delayed by almost 24 hours which barely made the 18 hour flight each way worth it, but we still went and we were literally in the air or at airports more than on the ground. As oddly as it may seem, I enjoyed every aspect of the trip and would do it again. Different than most travelers, I actually enjoy long flights because it gives me uninterrupted time to write, read, and catch up on movies I never make time to watch. When we finally touched ground, Jeff found it amusing that everyone else was eager to get off the plane, but I was disappointed that I had not yet completed all my writing projects or had the chance to watch my last movie while in the air. Singapore was amazing too!

Debbi and Mike have countless astounding and incredible stories of their varied world travels. Although they have spoiled themselves in the most desirable of vacations, their travels also included poverty-stricken, developing countries, some even without electricity. Debbi and Mike find beauty not just in picturesque gems of the world, but also in the struggles people face and overcome. These experiences have led them to appreciate the world in ways most travelers would never fully understand.

Deneen Andrades is a dynamic person with many gifts to offer. Along with her world traveling, she has written books for the purpose of healing others from the perspective of a Mental Agility Coach. She coaches clients on how to become a better version of themselves, both individually as well as publicly speaking in crowded lecture halls. Additionally, she consults for large corporations. As a transformational leader, Deneen had me write and record a theme song to be played for one of her speaking engagements promoting her book, **"Learning How To Pivot"**. Deneen is magical in the way she engages people and tells her story, listens to others, and finds the right words and motivational tools to help them. She is fortunate to have a career where she can travel the world and leave a positive influence on thousands of people. I admire and am inspired by her spirit. I encourage you to check out her website www.Deneen360.com for information in regards to her book and future speaking engagements.

Kathryn R. is an inspiration with her daily haiku writes of nature from her travels both locally and internationally. She is a beautiful, kind, sensitive, and spiritual soul. Kathryn is a retired history teacher which gives her a deep appreciation when traveling to places where the history is rich and meaningful. Our mutual interest in traveling the world and documenting our experiences for others to enjoy and learn from is definitely something that brought us together. We love to share stories and compare notes on places we have been or plan to go, and many places I mention in this book came about through our travel discussions.

I will now introduce a few of my family members who have either inspired me to travel and/or build community.

My mother, Bobbi G., had three different careers in her professional life: High school English teacher, travel agent, and after over three decades as a successful real estate broker, she retired. My father, Charles G., was an accomplished biochemist and a wonderful poet, an unusual combination. He was a brilliant man, whom I admired greatly. He loved people deeply and was chronically curious about the world. I am sure his creativity and enthusiasm for exploring and connecting with people was passed down to me.

Growing up, family dinners were important and the main way we stayed connected after our busy daily routines. We discussed our day at the dinner table and sometimes it led to playing board games or watching something interesting on television. We bonded on the weekends with fun day outings and memorable family trips.

All through their 55+ years of marriage, my parents enjoyed traveling the world together, but in the latter part of my dad's life, they were not able to do that. My father, passed in 2020 after a valiant struggle with Parkinson's disease. He never complained to others about his difficulties, and had an amazing spirit. His love for life and learning remained until the end. Thankfully, he had created wonderful memories with my mother before it became too difficult for them to travel together.

As for my mom now, she is very socially involved in her community and fortunate to be in loving relationship with a partner with whom she is exploring the planet once more. I know my father would be glad to know she is doing well and venturing out into the world again.

My brother Eric G. is an interesting person and is also very social, loves not only traveling, but living in different places for months at a time. He is a digital nomad, traveling freely while working online from anywhere in the world using technology as long as there is internet. Many digital nomads work in various places and move around to different locations like coffee shops or the beach. Digital nomad communities are communal environments where people may or may not work together. They live together with common areas like a living room/kitchen and attend to their business when they need to (*or want to*) and have the opportunity to socialize when not working. Some even set up group times to work alongside one another to relieve the potential isolation that this type of lifestyle can have.

Eric loves being able to hop around and experience new places and people and still keep his public relations career with this lifestyle. He also is one of the pioneering members of the media relations team for the annual Burning Man festival in the Nevada Black Rock Desert where people stay for a week or more with nothing but the food and accommodations they bring with them (*air conditioned RV if you're lucky)*. There is no money exchange, just gift economy. It is a real sense of community and acceptance for different lifestyles; anything goes. For most, it would probably be a culture shock, but for Eric, he thrives on that creativity and love for mankind (*as did my father*).

My daughter Rachel Johnston, has incredible leadership skills in growth promoting group activities she has created. Her craft workshops and educational group discussions, both in person and online, have made significant changes in people's lives. Although she works with all genders, she has branded herself as a women's self-love coach. Rachel has not traveled extensively, but does know how to bring a community together. We collaborate in leading a long-standing women's group and are excited to incorporate many of our ideas and exercises into group travel retreats as well. She is a great healer, speaker, and positive influence on others. Rachel has inspired me to pursue my dreams of starting group travel. She has a great way of holding people accountable once they make goals for themselves, as she has with me.

I know Rachel will definitely be an asset to my future retreats and I welcome her ideas and involvement. I encourage you to look up the various programs and activities that Rachel offers, both in person and remotely. Her **Instagram** information is **@_coachrachel** or she can be reached by email at **rachel_jhnstn@yahoo.com**.

Erin M. is a close friend that I essentially grew up with, as we met in high school when I was fifteen and she was sixteen and have been friends ever since. We have shared some crazy times such as Atari computer camp (a form of group travel) where we got in trouble and were sent home early for starting a food fight and buying alcohol under age, among other things. She was also the maid of honor in my first wedding. We have the kind of friendship where even if we don't talk for months, it feels like yesterday and the kind of connection where we could just look at each other and crack up laughing but can't really explain it. We connect on both a silly level and an intellectual one, at least as we became more mature that was true, but we still have our belly laughs and I absolutely love that about her. We both earned higher education degrees, my psychology doctorate and Erin with her law degree. We both have a love for traveling. Not only have we remained good friends, but her oldest son and my son are also friends and hang out together on occasion.

Erin, like my brother, has managed to find a way to not just be a tourist, but also "live" in other countries, and not just solo, but with her three sons. Erin, a single mother, wanted to teach her sons how to appreciate the world as a whole and expose them to different cultures. So she arranged to live in different countries for months at a time and homeschooled all three of them.

Erin emphasized the comparison between America and other countries (such as Southeast Asia) when it comes to living a healthier life and how medical coverage is more readily available and food is freshly picked and organic. She claims to have felt physically and emotionally healthier while living a simpler life.

In terms of group travel, Erin started TACI, the frisbee golf annual camping trip that has been going on for 30 years or so (pre-children). I will elaborate on what the acronym stands for, how it started, and what it involves in Chapter 6. Erin's interesting life of travel and connectedness to others has been very inspiring to me, and I am blessed to be a part of it all.

Susan Tate, wife of former Queensryche singer Geoff Tate, manager of his current band, **Operation: Mindcrime**, and founder of **Back Stage Pass Travel** (*more details in Chapter 6*) has an amazing story. I have learned an enormous amount from Susan in terms of what it takes to plan and manage group travel.

First of all, it was fascinating how she started Back Stage Pass Travel. Susan explains that she and Geoff have always loved to travel, just the two of them, with family, and with close friends. In her words, "We have these favorite places and took a couple of friends and one girlfriend said "you should take people on this trip because this is something nobody does". I started to talk and think about it for years with a lot of self-doubt "well what if people don't sign up"? I kept going back and forth about whether it will work and Geoff finally said, *(even if it doesn't work)* "it's only money, we'll make more" and "you either put this thing online or shut the fuck up". That must have been the clencher as, soon after, Susan starting finding people, fans of Geoff, on Facebook who regularly commented on Geoff's post and asked these fans (essentially strangers) out of the blue "Do you want to go on vacation with us?" To Susan's surprise, and disproving all the self-doubt she once had, it actually sold out in a day and she was overwhelmed with the huge response she received. The rest is history!

Because Geoff is still touring the world with Operation: Mindcrime, he and the band members travel about 90% of the time; that's over 340 days a year! Susan goes about 300 days a year. A number of trips that Susan attends, she plans with registered fans for a week at a time which she named Back Stage Pass Tours (BSPT). It is such an incredible experience to offer and what makes the opportunity particularly special is the music bond between group members along with getting to know a celebrity musician.

What I admire most about Susan is that she makes her trips very affordable and has converted many nontravelers into lifetime travelers. Although Jeff and I already were travelers before we went on our first BSPT trip, ever since, we have made BSPT a big part of our lives and have a new growing circle of friends. In fact, on page five of her Travel Agreement it reads, "<u>LIFE CHANGING FEELINGS</u> – Your life may be changed in ways that introduce you to a travel and/or music addiction. You may find yourself dreaming of faraway places and planning trips every chance you get. We encourage this and hope that we have given you a look at the world through the eyes of Geoff and the other musicians and it was everything you hoped for!" It actually brought a huge smile to my face when I read this because in our interview, Susan expressed how she's realizing what a responsibility it is to earn the trust of people to use their time and money they saved to travel with her. In the process she is changing lives, and she has changed ours.

Jeff and I have different music tastes. His favorite is heavy metal, mine is not but I will tolerate it sometimes. So when we went on our first Back Stage Pass tour, he disguised his lack of disclosure as a "surprise for me", but later revealed that it was because he feared if he told me what it was really about, I wouldn't want to go. He also said that I might enjoy the experience more than he will. Now that I have first-hand knowledge and understanding of Back Stage Pass Tours, I totally get both sides to what he was saying. Interestingly, I do really like Geoffe Tate's music, love all the band members, and think the fellow travelers are all wonderful people. What is most surprising and one of the things I am most thankful for is how much Jeff now likes group travel, so Susan has definitely changed our lives!

Ian McCartor, singer/songwriter, musician, retired traveling hospice nurse, and artist, is an extremely unique and talented individual whom I feel blessed to know and have as such an integral part of my life. Jeff and I first met Ian about eight or nine years ago on a music-themed group camping trip. It took a number of times running into Ian at various events and music circles for us to become future lifelong friends. Ian loves to travel and plans group retreats such as the castle in France, which I will detail in Chapter 6. Through Ian, I have met and gotten pretty close to seven or eight people that I now travel with, sometimes even without Ian!

Because Ian also worked for a hospice and was a traveling nurse for a period of time, it is no wonder he has tremendous compassion for others. I have cowritten and recorded a few songs with Ian and we are constantly sharing our creative contributions to the world every time we get together whether it be music, books, or the next retreat. I encourage you to check out this talented musician's work and different projects he is involved in at www.IanMcCartor.com.

CHAPTER 3

CATCHING THE TRAVEL BUG

I felt it appropriate to give credit not just to Jeff, my life partner, for reintroducing me to the world of travel after many years of putting it on hold; but also in my earlier, more formative years, to my parents who planted my curiosity of the unknown. They loved to travel and, although they did not always take me and my brother everywhere they went, we did get a sense of newness, learning about history and different cultures, as well as creating some of the best family memories we have to speak of today because of the experiences they provided.

Early Travel Experiences as a Child and Young Adult

Besides family visits in Florida, exploring our roots in New York, overnight summer camp for three weeks regularly, and many camping trips (both family and group), Mexico and Costa Rica are the two places my parents took us outside of the United States before we reached adulthood.

However, during childhood I did have the opportunity to travel further than those previous named destinations, just not with family. My first travel experience out of the country was when I was sixteen with my Jewish confirmation class and other temple groups on a trip to Israel. Although I am sure they were motivated to send me there partly for the educational benefit, I am 100% certain my parents were more about getting rid of me for not just three, but six weeks that summer! I am not just saying this to be funny, I have an actual story that proves it to be true. At one point during the trip (*probably week one*) I snuck away from the group with a friend to have a Shanti in a little side café when we got caught by our chaperone just as we were about to take our first sip! Apparently, he had been following us. When my parents were contacted about the incident of us "minors" breaking the American rules regarding underage drinking, they begged and pleaded the chaperone for me to stay regardless of my behavior (*because they desperately wanted me to be someone else's problem for a while*) and their wish was granted.

I certainly was a rebel in my youth. Another example in Israel was when I asked a Rastafarian if I could ride on his camel to the bus on which my peers were already waiting for me. It was hilarious to see their expressions while my head went bouncing up and down as I aligned with the bus windows and made my grand appearance.

There were around four bus-loads of teenagers exploring various regions of the Holy Land and it was, without a doubt, educational, adventurous, and fun. Other highlights were hiking Masada at 4:00am, putting a note in the Wailing Wall, eating chocolate (actually Nutella) on bread for breakfast, and floating in the salty Dead Sea. I remember learning some history and traditions especially while staying on a Kibbutz for a night. We also sang a myriad of songs with the group as we bonded over the six weeks. It was well planned and organized (*as it had to be in order to be safe and accommodating for well over a hundred rowdy teens, especially myself*). When I returned from that trip, my parents noticed a significant change in my outlook on life that I hadn't even realized. It was an amazing experience and I have vivid and fond memories of this trip that remain to this day.

Now, fast forward about 25 years! Life happened- college, grad school, marriage, children, career. As with most adults who take on multiple responsibilities at once, I have learned the true meaning of what "balance" is. I have juggled working full time with a very busy practice, active social life, singing in bands, and involvement in my children's extracurricular activities, dance competitions for Rachel and baseball practice and games for Josh. However, since I had so many competing responsibilities, I had to put off my desire to travel, at least until my children were a little older. Sure, we did some getaways as a family; Hawaii, Florida, Arizona, a few cruises, Disneyland, and camping trips, but it really wasn't until my 40's that traveling became a big part of my life.

A little late start as a world traveler, but "better late than never"! While you are physically and financially able, do not wait to travel once you retire like so many make the mistake of doing. A friend of mine waited too long to travel. Once he finally reached the end of his employment and was eager to reap the rewards of all those dedicated years, the stress on his body had already caught up with him and he unexpectedly perished the day after his retirement party. We are not promised tomorrow. I can never stress this enough. Now is the time and it waits for no one.

As soon as it was financially feasible, I cleared my work schedule to give myself the balance I desperately needed. Since doing so, I have never looked back, and never once regretted it. I also will never take these opportunities for granted. Every time I get on an airplane and take off above the clouds, I still am in awe at how amazing the experience of just doing that is. I am so fortunate to have the financial and physical freedom, and I hate to say it, but, I am fully aware those things could change in an instant.

The Beginnings of Many Overseas Travel Experiences in Mid-Life

To really "experience" (*albeit vicariously*) what goes through my mind as I travel, I fortunately captured these thoughts and feelings over a decade ago as I journaled on one of my trips. (I highly recommend documenting when traveling, rather than looking back and resenting that you had a missed opportunity). The following are a compilation of emails I wrote to friends and family, which I am now "cc'ing" you, the reader, into. They were written before and throughout my first of many trips to Europe I took back in 2011 with Jeff, with whom I have had thirteen years of great experiences.

In the beginning days of our traveling together, Jeff often had meetings in different countries (such as Thailand and Germany) and that would be an excuse to take me along for an extended trip. Since 2011, my traveling increased to 26 countries around the world and counting.

Enjoy this journey through five amazing countries. Accompany me in daily occurrences through the eyes of an optimistic psychologist. I will share what I learned, whom I met, and what I witnessed from funny and light-hearted stories to deep and heart-felt lessons.

Tues, 7/12/11

3 more nights and a wake up!! I wanted to send our trip itinerary:

Saturday, July 16, 2011 – Fly to Munich, Germany

(We happen to be flying on separate planes through different connecting cities so we depart in SD and reunite in Germany about 15 or so hours later)

Sunday, July 17, 2011 – Arrive in Munich, Germany

(Shower!!!!)

Monday, July 18, 2011 – Tuesday July 19, 2011 – Tour Munich while Jeff is in business meetings and enjoy night life together with his business partners. Planning to visit Dachau concentration camp probably Tuesday and whatever else seems interesting. I read about a place in Central Park where there is skinny dipping and river surfing.

Wednesday, July 20, 2011 – Leave for Salzburg, Austria
Ride bikes along the river and tour Mozart's birthplace

Thursday, July 21, 2011 – Tour sections of Austria and visit Salt Mines and ride the loge!!

Friday, July 22, 2011 – 1:34am train to Venice, Italy arriving 8:30am.

Saturday, July 23, 2011 - Depart for our 3 days in Tuscany Valley (wine country!) We have rented an apartment and will have a car in which to tour around.

Tuesday, July 26, 2011 – Leave for Lake Como (supposedly one of the most romantic places you can go!)

Wednesday, July 27, 2011 – Take train to Lucerne, Switzerland (Cheese fondue!)

Thursday, July 28, 2011 – Train to Lusanne, Switzerland and staying in Montreux where there is supposed to be great hiking.

Friday, July 29, 2011 – Evening train to Paris

Saturday, July 30, 2011 – Expect a picture of me in front of the Eiffel Tower.

Sunday, July 31, 2011 – Morning flight home.

A dream trip in the making!!! Just so you know, I have wanted to travel to Europe for almost 25 years and I am finally doing it!!! Please do not put off your dreams and aspirations as long as I did (no matter what it might be) because life is too short. I am so fortunate to finally be pursuing something I have only dreamed of doing. In case you can't tell, I am very excited!

Yours,

Stacy

San Diego Airport
6:10am Saturday, July 16, 2011

Sitting on the plane! I need to tell you though that in every trip there is always an "event" that takes place or funny situation that I find myself in even before I get to the airport. So, this time there were two things to write about. The first was my, on the verge, "panic attack". It only lasted about ten seconds but I felt myself panting and about to burst in tears when I couldn't remember exactly where I put my passport. I knew it was in my carry-on bag…somewhere, and at the end of those ten seconds of tossing things out of my bag came my passport flying out of my Europe book. Phew!!

The second event was on the way to the airport. My dear friend Lu Ann was kind enough to pick us up at 4:30 in the morning and in the car I asked Jeff which terminal we needed to be at, not realizing not only were we on separate planes and airlines, but that we were not even departing from the same terminal. Anyway, he said, with confidence mind you, that it was Terminal 2. We drove up and did not see United, which was where I needed to be! We dropped him off and rushed me back to my terminal where there were lines out the door, yes even on a Saturday at 5:00am. It all worked out obviously since I am now sitting on the plane. So (phew!) another sigh of relief! Bye San Diego! I will write again on my long layover in Chicago.

In flight from San Diego to Chicago
8:55 am (WST) Saturday, July 16, 2011

OK, I'm already very tired yet antsy, about ¾ of the way to Chicago, wondering if Jeff got free breakfast on his flight or if he had to pay $6 for a tiny ham and cheese croissant like I did. The banana I bought for a buck fifty at the airport didn't quite hold me over. It's strange how traveling seems to make you (*or at least me*) hungrier than usual. At home on my busy work days I can go through half to ¾ of a day before I feel "the need" to eat. I guess waking up at 3:00 am could have also had an effect on my early appetite.

Although I did have a significant role in planning our accommodations and some of what we will be doing in the different countries, I failed to be aware of my travel itinerary in terms of layovers and time changes. I am only mentioning this because I am realizing now how long of a trip this will be since, the way I figured, I woke up about six hours ago to get ready, am about fourteen hours away from landing in Munich, which means (*and as it appears on my plane ticket*) that I have a six -seven hour layover in Chicago. I was wondering what I was going to do with four hours! I am seriously debating whether to venture into Chicago for a brief visit as long as I can get a locker for my carry-on! I'll let you know.

Chicago O'Hare Airport

4:50pm CST Saturday, July 16, 2011

Waiting to board the aircraft now for the longer portion of the trip, although so far my layover in Chicago was longer than my airtime. I did not get out for fresh air after all for a number of reasons. First off, a nice gentleman overheard me talking on the phone about having a seven hour layover and offered to get me into the Red Carpet Room to wait it out! For those of you who don't know, it's a luxury waiting section for preferred frequent flyers where you get snacks, beer, wine, and luxurious seating, very nice. I hung out there for about half the time, and then lugged my heavy carry-on up and down the airport to get some walking in, wishing I had wheels on that bag.

As I approached my next gate it was bombarded with Asians flying to Japan, the flight out before mine. Now they are gone and the shift has changed to fair-skinned blue-eyed individuals. I feel like I have already been to two countries without even leaving the Unites States! Unless I have anything of interest to report, I plan on getting some ZZZ's on this next eight to nine hour flight so you will probably hear another update when I am *actually in* another country. Until then…

Well… I made it! Didn't get any REM sleep but did rest on and off. The flight from Chicago to Munich was slightly over eight hours. I was greeted just outside baggage claim by Jeff who arrived about an hour prior. As a side note and random observation, there was a dog at the airport and is it just me or has anyone else ever noticed that when you are in a foreign country it is not only the people that look unique. I swear this white poodle had a German face unlike any poodle I have seen! I guess it makes sense if you believe that a pet after a while tends to look like his or her owner. (*I mean compare my dog Emily and me…twins!! JK Anyway…*)

We rented a multi-van, were given a map, and the challenges began. First of all, it was a stick-shift which normally works well for Jeff however for some reason he had trouble with reverse and low gears up steep inclines. We started stalling and then rolling back on a ramp in the parking garage and almost hit the car behind us! It didn't really concern me until we got onto the autobahn. I envisioned the worst, but we were okay.

We also had to learn our way around and the map which was hard to navigate so, after 45 minutes of beautiful scenic driving, we finally turned ourselves in the right direction and arrived at our hotel. We got showered and are now waiting to be picked up by a local couple who are related to Jeff's mom's side of the family. I will let you know how our evening turns out.

Hotel room 2:25am Monday, July 18, 2011

Can't sleep!!! Aaah, don't you love the joys of jetlag and time zone changes? We were exhausted by 9pm last night because we had been up for 30 hours so I couldn't write then so here I am antsy to start my day now at this opportune time when everyone else is getting their shut eye. Hopefully after this entry I too will be able to fall asleep.

Last night was wonderful with our new friends Silke and Matthias in **Munich, Germany**. They were so accommodating and kind to us. They are both actors in their late 40's with twin 18 year-old boys. They picked us up at our hotel at 3:30pm and showed us all around Munich.

First we went to <u>Central Park</u> and watched the surfers in the river that I was hoping to see, very entertaining. Then we walked around the park and it started to rain on and off so we went into a coffee house and had apricot cheesecake and cappuccinos. We then walked all around old buildings and areas of Munich where history was made and discussed different things about the German culture. They reassured me that Germans are very good about educating youth about World War II and that there is a pretty substantial Jewish population here. Tomorrow I will be visiting the old grounds where the nearby concentration camp once was and will have more to say regarding this.

We were taken to a memorial for Michael Jackson which was very interesting. It was filled with photos and letters people wrote in his memory. I didn't find it surprising that he was so popular and loved by German people but what I did find surprising was that there seemed to be a sentiment that Michael Jackson was mistreated and disrespected and perhaps targeted as a victim towards the end of his life. There were statements posted about him not wanting to perform 50 shows that had been booked and that he was stalked and had his home raided without a search warrant and, once destroyed inside, he no longer considered it his home anymore.

One piece of literature stated resentment and anger about how bullies are causing the American Dream to be feared because of ridicule and accusations that go along with being famous (which this particular writer strongly believes Michael Jackson's case regarding the child molestation to be false and is under the opinion that he was being taken advantage of financially). His article talked about how unfair it is that someone so accomplished, talented, and philanthropic as Michael Jackson was, had to endure that kind of abuse. It ridiculed how he was heavily judged and criticized for being unique in his appearance and mannerisms. The title of the article was, "Does the American Dream Have to Die with Michael Jackson?" (Hubpages.com) Although I personally do not believe the American

Dream is dying, I found it interesting to see how the German culture (or at least a select few) views our media.

I also witnessed large swarms of teenagers who were very expressive in their dress attire, artistic in their makeup, varied in hair color, with a somewhat gothic yet not morbid, presence. They seemed very lively and happy as opposed to depressed or pessimistic. Although German people have a reputation of being reserved, I think many of the younger generation seem to be breaking away from that image. Perhaps one of the purposes of the writer mentioned above was to preserve this wave of creativity that not only youth here in Germany possess, but also youth everywhere else in the world.

After our Munch city walking tour, we met the twins at a wonderful Bavarian restaurant called <u>Spatenhaus</u> where I had roasted pork and dumplings (one potato and one bread). The bread dumpling will go on my list of favorite German foods now. It was delicious. I had to remind myself that there is no drinking age when I saw the two 18 year-olds not only getting served beer, but also being quite knowledgeable about the different types. When we all toasted each other, I noticed that everyone made eye contact one at a time and I prefer toasting the person versus the drink as well, which Americans in general do not tend to be conscientious of. I let them know I appreciated that.

On the way back to our car, two noteworthy events occurred. First, I almost got hit by a bicyclist. They are common here and although Silke kept warning me to beware, I had not yet got accustomed to walking on the left side of the sidewalk so the bicyclists can pass me on the right. If her brakes had not been as squeaky as they were, I would not have been aware enough to escape the potential tragedy that may have occurred. Although most times it is atrociously annoying, in that circumstance, thank god for squeaky brakes.

Secondly, there was some commotion involving policeman and a stopped trolley. Being the curious people we are, we walked over to find out what the situation was. We came to find out that a parked car was too far into the street to allow the trolley to pass. Therefore, the cart full of people riding the trolley were held up until they could either locate the owner of the car or have the car towed away. In all the years I lived in San Francisco with narrow streets and cable cars, I have never witnessed such a thing.

It is now 3:40am and although I still do not feel tired, I probably should leave you with some final observations then try to force myself to sleep at least until the sun appears. So, just so you know, the driver's steering wheel is on the left just like in the U.S. but the windshield wipers go in opposite directions rather than in unison, as opposed to here in America (*I think I sound more like a foreigner when I say "America" vs. "U.S." and I kind of like that*).

Here are some funny words Germans use instead of our terminology: "handy" for cell phone, "never lost" for GPS, and "big chicken" for … well I am not sure. Let me explain. This woman who was helping me interpret my lunch menu earlier today confirmed that the meat I was asking about was in fact chicken but then she self-corrected and said "big chicken". This left us not knowing if she actually meant an oversized chicken, or perhaps turkey or even duck (which is common here, as is "suckling pig" —which I am guessing could be a baby pig, I don't know). Nevertheless I will not likely find the truth of the matter since, after concerned contemplation, I opted for a steak. Good night!

Hotel room in Germany
1:07am Tuesday, July 19, 2011

I got a few more hours of sleep on and off and it seemed to hold me until now. Breakfast, especially the eggs here at the hotel, are terrific. Jeff says it's half and half they use instead of regular milk. It figures that all the bad stuff is what makes it taste so good and not only that but this is such a meat and potatoes kind of place that it has been hard to stick to my low cholesterol diet, although I am walking miles a day.

Once Jeff left for his meeting and I had another hour and a half nap, I ventured out to meet Matthias for more touring of Munich, but before I start with that, my transportation is worth noting. I took a cab first, which was only a two minute ride to the train station in Etchy and was told by the hotel receptionist to pay by credit card. I decided to pay with my cash Euros instead and did not get my change back, which ended up costing $15 US equivalency. When I asked about my change, the attendant mumbled something about tax and other things I didn't quite understand then she rushed me out saying my train had arrived. It actually did so I leapt out to hop on it, not realizing at that point that I had not bought myself a ticket, nor did I even take the time to check if I was on the right train!! When I confirmed that it was, I still was nervous about not having a ticket. Upon getting off the train, an English speaking woman told me I should have bought a ticket and that I may be fined 40 euro, (with the current exchange rate is about $56). I thought I could explain myself if need be but luckily as I looked up the staircase there was nothing to go through to get out so I managed to get to where I needed to be without the German police on my path! Anyway, I now know what to do and will plan better next time.

I had a wonderful tour of Munich. The most memorable part was he market place and I was about to witness a live fish flopping around about to be sliced alive!! I rushed out just in time telling Matthias that I really did not need to see that. We walked all over shops and an old church and then stopped to have afternoon cookies and latte. We had a very deep conversation about Nazi Germany and Hitler himself. He told me that his father was in the military at that time and that he later made a complete shift and became a priest. He told me that Jews are now very comfortable here because the majority of Germans who are old enough to understand feel responsible for making sure it never happens again. In fact, the laws are very strict when it comes to that now. I shared a story with Matthias about an individual somewhere in the Midwest who had a Nazi flag in his front lawn. It was controversial because of the discomfort it caused passersby and the dilemma about the right to free speech. I asked what would happen if this were to occur here in Germany and his quick answer was "imprisonment". They do not tolerate any such thing, which is comforting. It was a good orientation for my visit tomorrow morning to Dachau Concentration Camp.

After my day with Matthias, Jeff met me. We had a couple of hours getting lost in Munich then finally found our way to Hoffbrau House, where we met Matthias and Silke, and had another meat and potatoes meal. After, they took us to an elegant wine bar and upstairs was a restaurant all in the dark. I wanted to experience something similar in San Diego but that particular place had closed down before I had the chance to try it. Maybe next time I come to Germany I can experience that here, (although it will be doubly challenging to eat in the dark in addition to not speaking the language).

Before we left I went to use the "toilet" (the terms "restroom" and "bathroom" are not used here or anywhere in Europe). Anyway, I have a reason for sharing. I heard clicking in the hallway while in the stall and I had already questioned whether I was in the correct gender area because I don't always see the same wording or consistent symbols on the door to verify the gender *(to the reader, remember I wrote this content in 2011 so things were not as progressive with gender neutrality as in modern times)*. When after a few seconds, who I thought was a lady walking down the hall never entered the bathroom I chose, I really questioned whether I was where I should be. I quickly did my business and got out of there as quickly as I could, and as I was leaving, a man with the same clicking noise was coming up the hall from the other side *(where apparently the men's toilets were)*. Thank god for that. Without that universal picture of the lady with a triangle for a skirt as we have in the United States, it's hard to know whether I was in the intended area. *(As our world progresses, this scenario becomes a non-issue as gender neutral bathrooms or "toilets" are popping up everywhere).*

That is about it for today, however I did want you all to know, and you may think I am crazy but, I really did see a German version of my dog Emily today.

Goodnight!

Eching Hotel room, Germany
10:23pm, Tuesday, July 19, 2011

This is going to be a long one, I am warning you now, but please read every word of it. I want to start with our evening and end with the day. We just returned from a great dinner at a German Restaurant that is owned by a college that brews their own beer and has excellent food, called <u>Weihstephan</u> , located in Friesing. I ordered an orange tomato soup and the German mac and cheese (called "makkaroni und kase") and it was excellent. We sat on the patio and it was very nice until the thunder and lightning storms came. I have never seen lighting every 10 seconds with pouring rain for 45 minutes straight like that. We made it home safely though.

Now to my day…
I spent six hours in the **Dachau Concentration Camp**, one of the first Nazi concentration camps in history; mind you the history we are talking about here is only 66 years ago, shocking! The camp was in operation from 1933 to 1945, when it was liberated.

Let me first take you through the experience by telling you that initially Jeff was not with me due to a business meeting he needed to attend, so I was solo for the majority of the day. I rented an audio tour and learned and took in all I could. To describe the foundation of the facility, which was quite massive, my words will not do it justice but I will do my best.

As you enter the main iron gate surrounded by original barbed wire and six watch towers and you make a right there is a U-shaped building which was used mainly for administration purposes. It was where all prisoners were kept– Jews, Italians, French, Lithuanians,

Portuguese, Czechs, and other ethnic groups, as well as criminals, gays, and Jehovah's witnesses. Even the Nazi military who did not comply with Hitler's ways or tried to leak information about the reality of it all had been kept prisoner there. There were numerous people (besides the six million Jews) with different backgrounds who suffered for no justifiable reason.

They entered the building and were forced to give up all their identifiable documentation as well as their personal and sentimental valuables such as jewelry, pictures, and letters. Once checked in, they were assigned a number, some referred to it as their new "name". They had to strip down naked in a room full of other naked people (of course not with their loved ones since they separated men, women, and children in most cases never to be seen by one another again). Next, they got cleansed with harsh chemicals that burned and were shaven until they were bald, including the women. After this immediate humiliation and loss of dignity, they were asked to quickly put on the striped pajama uniforms and at times were forced to wear wooden shoes (which one prisoner stated, "it would have been fine if we had socks and if the shoes actually fit).

The first building was the museum portion of the tour that explained the political climate and the "false" premise of how the camp got away with becoming established at the time of the Second World War. People were desperate because of the economic crisis, and desperate times can lead to desperate measures, what I call "survival mode". Of course, many did not know what their fate would be until they were entrapped. If you were on the side of power, you followed orders to survive as the Nazi militia with complete emotional detachment. If not, their lives were in danger of becoming a prisoner themselves, which some of our heroes of the time did try to do. If you were a prisoner on the side of defeat, you did what you had to do to survive in order to avoid making the conditions substantially worse than they already were. Of course some had hope that someday they would make it out alive, although many were not strong enough to endure the conditions. Others chose to take their own life rather than having it taken from them. It was the highest level of cruelty and unimaginable circumstances they could fathom.

The growing number of overworked, overcrowded, starved, brutally beaten, sick with fatal diseases (like TB and malaria), subject to fatal inhumane medical experiments, or individuals simply shot or gassed and cremated became so overwhelmingly large. It required the creation of sub-camps to handle the growing atrocity. I was in awe viewing a map of hundreds of camps that I never knew existed and understanding how widespread it actually was. I knew about the bigger camps but had no idea of how much ground was being covered, and covered up for that matter (as these smaller camps did not bother keeping track of body counts as did the larger ones).

The museum tour ended with the explanation of how the truth was finally revealed leading to the liberation movement for those prisoners who were mentally and physically strong enough to survive the pure terror. Way beyond the administration building, you find the barracks where the prisoners were cramped onto wooden bunk beds. You also see acres of land once used for agriculture, the ditches where those who were lined up and shot fell to their death, and the area that really gave me my moment of sentiment.

Across a wooden bridge was the hidden place where the gas chambers and crematoriums were found. I walked through them and into the waiting room where prisoners were told they would be taking showers. Both rooms were later used to store 40,000 corpses awaiting the cremation process. I stood there today in the exact place where all this happened just over 60 years ago.

After four hours, Jeff was able to join me and was willing to have me give him a short version of the tour. What I thought would take us 30 minutes ended up taking us close to two hours, without even realizing it. What finally got me though was viewing those mass murder chambers the second time. We stopped to listen to an English speaking tour guide for a few minutes and, whatever it was that compelled me to stop and listen to her, I will be forever grateful. Her words resonated in me at that moment and still do. She asked the group what they could possibly tell others after viewing this unimaginable site of mass human destruction. She explained why she disagreed with the saying "never again" on one of the memorials. Her explanation was that it was "stupid" because this type of human destruction is still occurring in the world as we speak. She said, "it is not ignorance that got us here, it is apathy…"

I had to catch my breath for moment. She was so right. I took Jeff's hand in mine and walked down a shaded path of memorials and mass burials. These were human beings I never knew, and never will, whose bodies were disregarded and hidden. I felt so much empathy for them that I could not help but cry my eyes out. I told Jeff I got what I needed and my next reflections were: "if only people cared and cared enough, this may not have happened the way it did, and if only people today really care and care enough, it could stop happening now." I had a very moving day today and I wouldn't trade it for anything. I will definitely come back here- not just here to Germany, but here to this place in my mind, *my traveling mind*.

Peace

Zum Hershum Achat Hotel 12:05am, Thursday, July 21, 2011

We made it **Salzburg, Austria** after a long drive in the rain on the autobahn. Once in the city, we got so lost with the outdated paper maps that are so confusing to read. I told Jeff next time we come to a foreign country we NEED to get a "NEVER LOST" (GPS). He agreed. *(Although this was well over a decade ago and now our smart phones have plenty of capabilities so it is now another non-issue).*

We walked in the rain all day around beautiful Salzburg, meandering through gardens with an old castle view in the background. I like the unpredictable nature of the roads not being on a grid as they are in most cities. You drive for a while and all of a sudden make a sharp turn and a circular movement. You pass through some awesome looking eateries, then back to the main street again.

Salzburg is actually a lot bigger than we anticipated. The people are nice. I bought some Mozart Balls to bring home. This is the birthplace of Mozart; I didn't know before we researched where to go on this trip. The highlight of this day, was the evening. I had booked us tickets to a classical Mozart music/opera dinner show. We were seated with two other couples and a single woman. One couple was from California and Canada. One was from Russia. The single lady was from California but for the last six years she has been teaching elementary school children in Kuwait. I find such interesting people when traveling. I love it! This schoolteacher told us interesting things about Kuwait, but her overall opinion was that although it was very safe, she found it boring, dusty, and hot. She works mainly to be able to travel. The wealthy people have more money than they know what to do with. The women are allowed to drive and wear what they want, but still have nannies taking care of their children. She elaborated that these children may be twelve and still not know how to tie their own shoes. They do not utilize dental care either apparently. Anyway, enough about Kuwait, that is not where we are now, right?

Tomorrow we have an exciting day planned. We are getting picked up at 9am by Jeff's brother's old exchange student and her parents to go to ice caves and salt mines. We then go out to the country where they live and take a 12:30am sleeper train to Venice.

Zum Hirshen Achat Hotel in Salzburg, Austria
7:10am, Thursday, July 21, 2011

I am writing again this morning because I failed to mention that the restaurant and concert hall we were in last night was actually the oldest building in Europe and the actual place where Mozart himself performed. It was called <u>St. Peterstifskeller</u>. It had high, painted ceilings and it was beautiful.

Secondly, I wanted to mention that the hotel rooms we stayed in were very homey with a lot of character. Wood floors are common as opposed to carpet, which gives it a rich feel. Buildings tend to be older so it does not have that modern retro look, but rather a comforting serene and quiet feel that's hard to describe. It's almost like the building has been around for so long that it takes on a life of its own. It must know something you don't.

I also wanted to say that after spending four to five days in two German speaking countries, I have picked up a few words. Here they my favorites: <u>Ausfahrt</u> (means exit off the autobahn which is their word for "freeway" and it does not mean exiting gas from your behind ..haha), <u>Nein</u> (pronounced "nine" means no), <u>Prost</u> (what you say when you are toasting a person). Coming here the only word I knew was <u>Danke</u> (thank you). I need to get showered up and ready for our long, but exciting day, so until we meet again... Be happy.

12:14am Friday, July 22, 2011 on the train from Linz, Austria to Salzburg

I am writing this from a train on the way back to Salzburg where we have nine minutes to board the next sleeper train that will take us on a seven hour ride to Venice, Italy. We got picked up at our hotel by Nadine, who was an exchange student for two and a half weeks and lived with Jeff's brother, his wife, and three kids. Her parents also joined us. We got into their sedan (five-seater, Europe generally has small cars, not SUV's) so with all our luggage we were at full capacity for a long ride to **Halstatt**, Austria where the salt mines were. It was maybe a little too cozy, but it felt comfortable. Along the way we made a few stops to see where Nadine's father performed (he is a musician) as well as places to snap beautiful photos. Also I was low on my eyebrow pencil and Nadine assisted me in finding what I needed. We were lucky the rain finally had some mercy on us and we had a dry and pretty pleasant day.

We arrived in the gorgeous town of Halstatt. It was everything I had read and seen from pictures. We rode up a cable car and hiked a beautiful trail to the top, put on our garb (which looked like a nursing uniform, mine was green and Jeff's was orange) and had a blast sliding down fast slides! Our fastest speed was 32 km per hour! We learned interesting facts about the miner's life 7,000 years ago. I was in awe about how old Europe's history is compared to relatively young American history.

To Americans, if a building is celebrating its 100th or even 50th birthday, it's a big deal. In Europe, that wouldn't be very impressive. The ice cave we went to after the salt mines was ten million years old! Back to the salt mines, I was also in awe of how huge the cave was – the biggest I had ever seen – you could walk in it for miles. It was also the first time I read subtitles out of necessity. Usually it's by choice while watching a foreign movie. So, that was a different experience.

In both caves the tour guides spoke German (Austrian dialect is slightly more soft than German dialect I noticed). Luckily they repeated themselves in English to accommodate the minority of us that were American. I remember being annoyed when people started talking amongst themselves so that we couldn't hear unless we moved up to the front when the guide was speaking in our language and not theirs. I will now be more sensitive to people struggling with English who took the time to travel far to see and learn about our country.

When the salt mine tour was over, we got to ride a train that you had to straddle in order to reach the outside. It was such a fun experience. By now we were getting pretty comfortable with the family and Heidi (Nadine's mom) loves to sing so, quite naturally, we had a bonding moment when she and I started singing a Mozart tune together and I got it on video. This was one of those moments where you realize music and nature can bring people together in a universal way without even speaking the same language.

We were hungry after the salt mine tour so we went into a village and had a traditional Austrian lunch. I ordered a meat strudel soup (which I love!) and tried the well-known <u>Wienerschnitzel</u> – lightly breaded pork, with German potato salad. The next experience we had in Austria was the ice caves, and although not as interactive, they were incredibly beautiful and impressive. Prior to entering them we also got to ride a cable car up but it was not on a track, just the cable, and it hung and swung a little at times but just glided up that mountain so smoothly. They (*and I don't know who the "they" that is responsible for this is*) didn't mention that our fifteen minute walk the rest of the way up was actually a pretty strenuous hike. However, as exhausted as it made us (well Nadine, Heidi and me anyway, as Jeff seems to glide up the mountain as easily as the cable car), it was worth the effort and the views!

After we were done touring both caves, we had a two hour drive (now in pouring rain) to their hometown. We had dinner at their friends' agricultural farm bed and breakfast "mansion". It has several eating rooms, an indoor pool and sauna, and several rooms with private bathrooms you could rent. Jeff and I are interested in going back to stay there. It is one of the vacation spots of Sylvester Stallone, we are told. Anyway, they served what they called a platter of "cold" dishes (but it was actually room temperature) and we all shared them (the five of us plus Nadine's brother and boyfriend). The platter consisted of various meats and cheeses, dark bread with three different spreads. It was delightful but maybe not something we would do every night for dinner since a hot meal is what we are accustomed to.

We then went to Nadine and her parent's home, which was only five minutes away and they thoroughly took pleasure in showing us around. Heidi is an interesting and very funny woman. She does mind, body, and soul remedies, such as body cleansing and massage therapy. After touring her beautiful home, we enjoyed our last moments and giggles with the family. They served delicious Austrian desserts and tea. Regardless of our language barriers, we felt close. We found humor in the hand gestures we each came up with when we could not articulate our point in words. It was an incredibly warm and welcoming atmosphere and they made us feel like family. I believe this will not be the last time we spend together. We were welcomed back and certainly encouraged them to visit us if they ever planned on being around our neck of the woods. Today was a wonderful day from every angle. Tonight we sleep on a train and wake up in Italy.

Written in lobby of our Venice Hotel near San Marco Square at 7:50pm Friday, July 22, 2011

The sleeper train was surprisingly nice. We were treated like royalty because we didn't have a "second class" ticket. We got the most expensive which was the private cabin with beds that fold out (bunks), a sitting area, closet, and vanity area with a sink. We had the curtain open when it was still light to see the gorgeous views, but once it got dark, we could not see when the next station was coming. One time the train suddenly came to a stop with the bright lights shining in our cabin while doing my nightly routine of brushing our teeth only wearing my night shirt and underwear. We laughed at the fact that we had an unexpected audience.

We managed to get some sleep and I woke up with the extreme giggles again because the porter knocked a few times to bring our breakfast and all I could hear was Jeff clicking the lock, unlock, lock, unlock knob and swearing every time because he couldn't figure out how to open the door. I guess for this one, you had to really be there.

After disembarking from our train, we ventured off to find our hotel. What seemed simple proved not to be as we found ourselves lugging two heavy wheelers with our carry-ons on top for quite a while. The streets in **Venice** are cobblestone and, again, no grid blueprint, so not easy to understand. An added challenge are bridges with steps up and down every quarter of a mile. Whenever we would stop and ask for directions and show someone the name and address of our hotel (Best Western San Marco Plaza), they would just point in a general direction and tell us it was about ten more minutes. My legs hurt and my hands were getting callous. I noticed my mood changing from being elated about finally being in Italy, to becoming cranky. I certainly didn't want this to be my first memory of Venice. We tried to get a water taxi but, as were the trains leaving Venice, they were all on a 24 hour strike. There are no cars in Venice so we had no choice but to tough it out. There are porters that will take your bags so you can walk unburdened but they are hard to come by. As unique and interesting as Venice is, you must learn to take the great with the "not ideal".

Once we finally go to our hotel room after an hour of walking, we were obviously happy to arrive. It was still morning so we couldn't check in, but we gladly left our bags with the attendant. We then walked around and got pizza, a glass of wine for me, and coffee for Jeff. We checked in around 2:30pm and I completely passed out for a three hour nap, which is partly why I fell so far behind in my writing and emails. I guess I really needed the rest.

On our way to dinner we saw an interesting sight. We had seen these men from Ghana trying to sell "so-called" brand name purses on the street and at one point, one called out "policia" and, like a herd, they all took off running for their lives, or livelihoods, as quickly as humanly possible. It was definitely something to see and wished I had captured it on video.

We went to a very nice dinner next to the Grand Canal called <u>Restaurante Raffalle</u> where we saw gondolas and boats pass by. We had our second gelato after dinner and walked some more and are now back at the hotel. Tomorrow we explore Florence and then Tuscany. Goodnight.

2:40pm Saturday, July 23, 2011
Sitting on the Train to Florence

Our train ride has been a little chaotic because we weren't aware that the seats were assigned and had to move not once, but twice. The first time we were just in the wrong seats, the second time we realized we had the right seat but in the wrong car. Anyway, we are settled now for the remaining hour of our trip. I look forward to checking in with you this evening after we get settled at our little apartment in Tuscany!

Bye for now! Stacy

12:20pm Sunday, July 24, 2011
Balcony in **Tuscany** near Sienna

Florence was nice but we only saw a small portion and basically stopped for lunch, so I need to report more about it at a later point. We then headed toward our Agriturismo Malafrasca and it took us over an hour of getting lost (as usual) and asking people who speak no or little English, but when we finally got here, just before dark luckily. (Since people seem to understand my limited Spanish as opposed to my English, I am starting to speak Spanish so I can be understood.) It is beautiful, out in the country, very private, hardly anyone around, and they make their own wine here and gave us a complimentary bottle. The wine is so inexpensive here so we are planning to bring some back as well. After getting settled with a late dinner in the village, we called it a night.

Today we will be exploring Siena followed by the wine county of Chianti and hopefully getting a tour there. Tomorrow our plan is to go to Cinque Terre (an area of five small villages on the Mediterranean Sea). The next day we are getting up early to take a train to Lake Como. I will write this evening to let you know how today was. Miss you all.

Stacy

Agriturismo Malafrasca in Siena
11:03pm Sunday, July 24, 2011

Today we ventured into <u>Siena</u>, in the Tuscan region of Italy. We had to take care of business partly to pay for our accommodations since they prefer cash. After getting lost once again, we did manage to find a bank and some sights to see but somehow ended up on a "traffico limitado" area and were the only car on this pedestrian-filled narrow street. I am sure people were not happy with our Fiat trying to work its way through the crowds. There have been many times on this trip that I felt like a "dumb American" and I don't particularly like that.

I have been telling Jeff that when we go places to try not to make it obvious we are tourists by carrying a map and saying "Thank you" versus "Danke" or "Gratzi" or whatever the native language happens to be. It makes it more fun to try to fit in, versus to stand out like a sore thumb. Anyway, we finally made it out of the uncomfortable situation we found ourselves in and entered into another driving situation. This time, we just happened to be caught in the middle of something we had nothing to do with, and were just at the wrong place at the wrong time. We entered into a parking lot and, before we knew it, found ourselves trapped in between two cars with men disputing about who had the right to the parking space. They were arguing in Italian and one had his wife holding a spot after they had claimed to be driving around for two hours, while the driver behind us was arguing that it should have been his spot. We did not want to cast our votes, just wanted to get out of there and find somewhere else less chaotic to park and get some lunch. I finally got out of my car and told the man ahead of us "Yo comprendo pero we need to leave!" He did respect our wishes and we made our quick getaway. I managed to get some of the altercation on video since it was rather amusing.

We finally found a local restaurant and it was pleasantly surprising. First of all, we got to park right in front of the restaurant. Secondly, the crowd was fun to watch since half of them were into the car racing event being broadcast on television. Thirdly, the food was superb. We then ventured out to the Chianti countryside and were trying to find a particular winery that gave a 4:00pm tour and, although we arrived early, no one seemed to know about it. Two young Finnish couples came and were expecting the same tour but nobody came out or even answered the phone. We chatted with the Finns for a while, then continued on our journey. We stopped through Radda and then a very nice hotel resort called <u>Ill Borgo di Vescine between Radda and Castellina.</u> We tasted wine there, and since it seemed like no actual wineries were easy to find, it was nice to get some individual attention from a wine connoisseur in this beautiful location we just happened upon.

After wine tasting, we stopped in the village of Castellina and had a wonderful dinner there. I had the best baked cheese (Pecorino) with honey I had ever had coupled with ravioli with cheese, spinach, and meat sauce. We then enjoyed the sunset ride home and got settled for our big day out to the Mediterranean Sea tomorrow morning. I am tired and need to rest because we are forcing ourselves to get up early since we have a two and a half hour drive each way.

Night and enjoy the rest of your weekend what is left of it!

Stacy

7:30am Monday, July 25, 2011
Agriturismo in Siena

The Importance of GPS When Driving in Foreign Countries

We are about to leave on a two and a half hour (at least I hope no longer) road trip to the coast, Cinque Terre, and I wanted to mention that when choosing a partner in general but particularly a travel partner, one must be aware of one's own levels of tolerance. Tolerance of frustration and disappointment when things are not as you expected, tolerance of extreme heat or cold, tolerance of hunger when you are not conveniently at a food destination. If I was here without a GPS with anyone else I may have been counting the days to come home.

Jeff is a patient person and will go along with whatever plan that I am excited about, throws in a few of his own ideas, and pretty much goes with the flow. He always says, "I'm not worried about anything." (Although I will tell you he was pretty stressed when he was driving through pedestrians, and didn't like that I found it sort of comical. He was seriously worried about hitting someone given he still struggles with the stick shift when it is stop and go traffic). So besides his frustration with me finding humor in things he may take more seriously, we are a pretty good team. The other things I get annoyed with (in addition to when he doesn't try to speak the language or makes it obvious we are tourists) are things that are conditional with traveling so once we're home it will be null and void.

As much as I don't necessarily want people to know or treat me like an American when I travel overseas, there is no way to hide that fact. It isn't that I am not proud to be an American. (I do receive satisfaction when I tell someone I am from California and their eyes light up.) It's just that I don't want to feel (although I know I am) just passing through as a temporary visitor. It's challenging, especially when we do one-nighters, but even for the short bits of time that I am in a different place in which I never laid eyes on, have any history with, or even knew existed, I like to get a true sense of what locals experience every day. It's impossible to accomplish that when you are carrying a map in one hand, a camera in the other, and asking people if they speak English because you are lost. I admit I have been that person a few times myself, and sometimes you just can't avoid it. I encourage anyone, wherever you go, to take in what's there, but more importantly, to avoid hours of going in circles and having unusual thoughts of causing pain to someone you love, make use of our modern technology and bring a GPS! (*Or in today's world, simply a smart phone*).

10:05pm Monday, July 25, 2011
Written in the car driving back from Cinque Terre, Italy

We just enjoyed a full day driving to <u>Cinque Terre</u>. It was beautiful once we arrived, but of course we got lost prior and took a detour through Lucca. We mainly hung out and had lunch in <u>Vernazza</u>, a nice coastal town where they have an old castle we climbed up. Surprisingly, out of every place in the world, we ran into someone Jeff knew! It was an ex co-worker from his old company and her family. What a small world it really is!

On our way back we took a different route through <u>Volterra</u>, a very cool village on top of the mountain built on a huge ruin site that is well-preserved with ample amounts of wine bars, restaurants, and shops. It had more night life than we have seen thus far in Italy, including Venice. We had dinner in a restaurant that was recommended by Antonella (the lady we met while wine tasting in her wine and cheese shop who let us sample my new favorite cheese - pecorino). Once we found the restaurant, which was in walking distance and not hard to find, we sat at an outside patio table with two other couples surrounding us and placed our order. Our meal consisted of steak (which was the second time I ordered steak this whole trip since I was not impressed with the steak in Germany), a salad, baked spinach with garlic, and risotto with cheese and sausage. It was fabuloso!!

After a while we were laughing because the risotto did not come out and we were just about done eating. I reminded the waiter about the order and as he brought it out, I joked, "dessert". The lady and her husband sitting across from us were laughing with me so I started talking a conversation. She was from Belgium and her English was good. We started talking about the places we each were going. The younger couple across from us was just sitting back and listening and I wanted to include them so I asked them where they were from. It just so happened that they were from the same small town in Belgium that the first couple was from. I shared about our similar coincidence earlier today with Jeff's coworker and soon after that it seemed as though Jeff and I were X-ed out of the conversation, or at least we no longer understood a word of it. Again, I felt like a "dumb American", but what I should focus on is the fact that I may have brought these people together who apparently had a lot in common. That feels good even if I had less in common with them. There are so many opportunities like this when you travel to reach out and connect with others and some of these connections are short-lived and temporary while others can be life changing and ever-lasting. There was nothing wrong with how today unfolded (besides getting lost, but that was okay too). We had a terrific day and evening.

On the drive home from there through the countryside, we had to stop for a herd of cows crossing the road at their leisure. It was awesome!!

Ciao for now.

2:05pm Tuesday, July 26, 2011
Nuova Miralago Hotel
(Bellagio) **Como, Italy**

We have covered so much ground on our trip and by so many means of transportation. We flew to Germany (obviously), and then it was a variety of trains, busses, cars, boats and ferries. We have covered large cities (both modern and medieval), small towns and villages, countryside with rolling hills, tunnels, bridges, waterfalls, and majestic mountains. We saw the ocean and the great sea, as well as smaller, calmer bodies of water. Where we are now is sort of a combination. We are staying one night on Lake Como at a Bed & Breakfast (my first one ever!). There are cars, scooters, and motorcycles allowed here (unlike Venice), and ferries seem to be the next popular means of transportation. People actually drive their cars onto the ferry to transport them to the other side of the lake or any of the other ports since driving between them is either impossible or dangerous.

Bellagio, out of all the ports on Lake Como, seems to have the most to offer in terms of restaurants and shopping. It is classy and beautiful. The lake is large with quiet ports and busier ports with ferries, water taxis, and speed boats. You cannot swim in the lake however.

We woke up at 5:30am and left Tuscany at 6:30am, drove an hour into Firenze (nobody here calls it "Florence"), then took an 1 and a half hour train to Milan (more modern fashion conscientious city) then an hour train to Como. We then cabbed it to the ferry station and took a 40 minute ferry to Bellagio. We were then told to wait "ten minutes" (the standard Italian answer for how long things take) for another taxi to our hotel (*I was NOT about to drag our luggage across town again!*). All in all it was about a seven hour commute door to door. This is not the way we would plan a one night trip back home but we are touring the land so we make exceptions. Tomorrow morning we need to catch a ferry and taxi then a three hour train with one connection to Luzern, Switzerland. I know…. We are doing a lot of running around but at least there will be no more driving without a GPS for the remainder of our trip! What I like about moving around so much is the variety of culture and scenic landscaping we have experienced.

11:00pm Tuesday, July 26, 2011
Hotel at Bellagio

I love **Bellagio**. It feels very comfortable with a hint of familiarity (although I have never been here before). Maybe because it seems a little more modern than some other places in Italy. It has a contemporary feel and there are lots of wine and cheese tastings. It offers a luxurious lifestyle and seems like a fun place to live. I would definitely want to come back and visit again.

My ankle seems to be giving me some grief today and Jeff bought a bandage to keep it more stable in the miles of walking we do every day. I hope to be okay because we have two days of touring Switzerland and one full day and two evenings in Paris left to go. I never knew how much walking I would be doing in Europe and I chose to mostly wear my flip flops. You live and learn.

We had a nice day walking around Bellagio, met a couple from Scotland while sipping on wine. We then had dinner and it was delicious (as is all Italian restaurants we've been to). I had a chicken Parmigiana type dish. Jeff had trout. As a side note, I have been trying to find a place to try pesto before leaving Italy but it either was not on the menu or, if it was, the few places included walnuts in their recipe and didn't want to chance an allergic reaction.

After dinner we went to a really neat wine bar that was carved out of a cave and walled with hundreds of wine bottles sticking out. There we met a nice couple from Ireland and Australia. Another couple was more into wine tasting than I had ever seen, the way she held up the glass and closed her eyes for at least a minute as she smelled the aroma; it was as if she was making love to the wine, funny. Speaking of funny, the last table in the room of four tables was occupied by a young woman and two men. They were laughing first because they had spilled some wine on the floor by accident, but it turned into hysterical laughter over who knows what. Since laughter is universal, not language-specific, and quite contagious, I found myself laughing with them even though I had no idea what was so funny. Fun stuff, I will miss Italy but I know it is a place I would love to visit again.

1:35pm Wednesday, July 27, 2011

We are on the beautiful train to Luzern, **Switzerland** going through the <u>Swiss Alps</u>, and this time it is daylight, unlike when we were on the sleeper train going through the Austrian and Italian Alps. Last night I think I ate something that didn't agree with me but it isn't too bad. I am hanging in there. Ready for some cheese fondue!!

Ciao

3:20pm Wednesday, July 27, 2011

We made it to Luzern, Switzerland but not without incident. Jeff couldn't print the ticket he bought online so at the train station we were told to board on an earlier train to the next station where we would have 10 -15 minutes to deal with the ticket issue before boarding the train we needed to take for our transfer city Lugano, Switzerland. We barely made it, but made it nonetheless.

Once we arrived, I needed to get francs since Switzerland is the one country in Europe that has not conformed to using the universal currency, Euro. A few places will accept Euros, but it's best to have francs just in case. Getting a taxi was no problem but Jeff accidently booked the hotel for the night prior. Luckily they had a room for us. Although all that may sound stressful, and it was at the time, it was nothing compared to driving without a GPS! I think I could handle almost anything else that comes our way now.

So far we really like **Luzern**. Here they speak mostly German and French it seems. Getting out of our taxi, we met an older lady who said she lived in La Jolla, California for 18 years and now lives in London. She went on about how all her friends in San Diego area never travel and just play golf all the time and she could not understand that. She is an avid traveler and gave us some nice ideas for our stay here. One suggestion was funny. Apparently there is a coffee shop at the end of our hotel block that is actually a brothel but you would never know it. She told us how amusing it has been for her to sit there and watch innocent people or even families with children go in and become shocked at the solicitation they received and dress apparel of the waitresses. I joked with her, "well if my boyfriend tells me later this evening that he is going down the block to get a cup of coffee and does not return for a while, I will know what's up!"

We are planning to walk around town this afternoon, hit the hot spots (not necessarily the one mentioned above), and find this highly recommended Fondue restaurant for dinner. Tomorrow our plan is to take a cable car up Mount Pilatus and possibly ride a luge if it doesn't rain. After that we have a two nd a half hour train ride (more time to write!) to our next destination Montreux, Switzerland where there is a castle called Chateau de Chillon. It is a well preserved castle from the 13th century, and it has a dungeon and 700 year-old toilets! Speaking of which, I seem to be just fine now!!

As I am sitting here looking out the window waiting for Jeff to finish his emails, I saw a family (mom, dad, and two daughters) riding down the street on bikes with strap-on back-packs. What a European way to travel. Europeans are adventurous and they do not seem to mind walking up steep hills, or in many cases do not have a choice, unlike Americans who can be spoiled by all the modern conveniences. Speaking of which, I have not seen any video arcades or children using game devices while out and about. They seem to be content with just being with family and not needing all the devices that take people away from people. Just an observation.

7:10pm Wednesday, July 27, 2011

We just walked around in the rain, yes again! I was so unprepared for this weather and was tired of wearing flip-flops and the same one pair of clean"ish" jeans I had left, so I bought myself a pair of European jeans. They are J-Wells, not familiar with the brand, but always wanted a pair of European jeans. I also really needed different shoes for the rain and wanted boot type shoes for winter so I found some unique boot-ish shoes that suit me well. Finally, I feel a little more put together now than I felt before as I stroll the city streets. I also bought some Swiss treats and chocolates of different types (to add to the Austrian chocolate collection I purchased last week).

We found the <u>Fondue House in Luzern</u>, which was the one recommended, serving three courses of fondue – cheese, broth for meats, and chocolate. My tummy is growling with excitement so until later...

12:11am Thursday, July 28, 2011

We had the most awesome dinner at the Fondue House in Luzern. We ate so much it was hard to walk back to the hotel. I had mentioned before that I was surprised about the lack of night life there was in the cities we have visited. Luzern is definitely the liveliest out of all the places we have been. On the way back, while we were crossing one of the bridges, we ran into some Russian people having a good time, and in my jovial, silly mood, as they were taking a picture I put up rabbit ears behind one the guys' heads. Luckily they had a good sense of humor and we all laughed. They offered to take our picture, and without Jeff being aware, I made rabbit ears behind his head. When the Russians returned our camera to us they were eager to see Jeff's reaction when he viewed it to see if it came out. We all laughed. One of the guys even took our picture with his own camera because they were amused. Again, another example of how laughter can bring strangers together. I love it.

3:20pm Thursday, July 28, 2011
Sitting on a train toward Lausanne and then to Montreux, Switzerland

We had a fantastic day today. We spent our time exploring <u>Mt. Pilatus</u>. Getting there was fairly quick and easy once we figured out which platform our bus was leaving from. We went through town and had a nice five minute walk where we saw houses with goats and sheep in their backyards. We got to the cable car lift and took it ¾ of the way up and rode the toboggans! I don't know what the difference is between a luge and a toboggan but we each sat in our own and it went down twists and turns down a metal slide. It was the longest one in Switzerland. We were lucky to be able to ride it at all because just as we were about to buy our ticket it had started to rain at the bottom, even though we couldn't tell from up top, and apparently you cannot break when the slide is wet so they had to close it down indefinitely. Anyway, we waited about 20 minutes or so and finally the rain stopped and we were able to ride.

It was amazingly fun and even after the ride you just get to sit back (backwards actually) as you get towed up the mountain again. An added bonus was passing by grazing cows about three feet away from you. It was beautiful scenery as well. There is nothing quite like it in the states that I know of. We were also very fortunate to get a free second ride since we had to wait so long due to the rain. We took the opportunity of course to enjoy it a second time, where our bravery allowed us to cruise faster than the first time. Thrilling! It started to sprinkle again on our way back up and when we reached the top, they had closed it down again. I guess it was meant to be for us!

Next we rode another cable car up to the tip top of the mountain. We were 7,000 feet high! The views were phenomenal. We were actually above the clouds! There was a cave we walked through and we learned that people actually believed there were fire-breathing dragons living there years ago. They had a few restaurants and even two hotels at the top.

We got back to the bottom, hopped on the bus just as it was pulling up, and decided that we had just enough time to catch the 3:00pm train if we hurry, as opposed to the 4:00pm train. Jeff offered to run back to the hotel (four to five blocks away) with a 20 minute window to grab our two wheeler suitcases and carry-on bags along with his computer backpack. I waited nervously at the pretzel place, and when I heard him call my name about five minutes to 3:00pm I was relieved! We made it just in time. I will update you on Montreux when I have more stories to share.

Ciao for now.

11:00 pm Thursday, July 28, 2011
Golf Hotel Rene Capt
Montreux, Switzerland

We got here early evening and had a very nice taxi driver tell us all we needed to know. It is a beautiful place, right on Lake Geneva, with the castle just a 15 to 20 minute walk along the river. We can see it from here. We walked into town once we got settled and found a very nice restaurant called The Chateau overlooking the lake and we both ordered fish. Jeff ordered trout again and liked it better here than the other night in Italy. I ordered a lake fish that was a Swiss combination between trout and salmon. It was prepared with crusted almonds and it was delicious. We have been eating very well. Thank god we are walking a lot every day, whether we plan to or not, it just happens.

Europeans have a different concept than Americans do about what is considered "walking distance", let me tell you. We would never even consider walking the distances that Europeans say is an easy walk, "ten minutes". Usually those supposedly quick walks end up taking us at least a half hour or more, partly because we get lost and typically only have a gist of where we're headed. The other part is they do not mention that these "easy" walks are not that easy when they involve steep hills or many stairs to climb. Most of Europe is not flat, it is very hilly. It's all good though. We need the exercise with all we have been consuming.

The other thing I have been noticing throughout countries is that dogs are very popular and welcome here. I know I've alluded that they perhaps look more human-like than American dogs, but they also seem to be treated more like people. They are taken everywhere; to the bank, to restaurants, you name it. You know I love my dog Emily, who is doing very well I am told, and she accompanies me to work and helps heal my clients alongside me just about every day. Jeff loves dogs too and has been making a lot of dog friends here. He says he likes dogs more than people, and I think that is mostly true.

Well that was our evening. I will tell you all about the castle next and afterwards we will be off on a train to Paris for our last two nights!

1:30pm Friday, July 29, 2011
On the speed train to Paris, France

We had a nice buffet breakfast at our hotel this morning, which by the way, had the best service out of all the hotels thus far, and we only have one left to go. We felt like royalty –were given a map and directions to points of interest without even having to ask, were given bus cards to ride the local bus with unlimited rides into town or the castle, and the breakfast buffet was included along with quality cappuccinos and lattes. It had a garden in the back with a great location along Lake Geneva. The pathway behind the hotel took you to town where we had dinner. If you followed the path in the other direction, it led to the castle with gorgeous flowers, boats, and beautiful homes along the way.

I forgot to mention in my last email how nice the hotel was in Montreux so I felt it deserved some mention, although I must say (*half-jokingly*) that the best part was that there were no stairs to climb with our heavy luggage. I do want to also note however, that all of our accommodations were wonderful in their own way. They were all clean and had all the necessities we needed, not one disappointed us.

You are probably wondering about the <u>Castle de Chillon</u>. It was interesting, beautiful, and would be easy to get lost in the maze of tunnels, rooms, and steep (and sometimes narrow) spiral staircases. I got to see the "latrines" (French word for toilets), which were actually wood panels with holes in them, which emptied into the lake below. There, of course, was no plumbing in that era. We saw the prison where one man in particular was held captive due to dissenting from the Savoy family and was kept in isolation from people and landscape views for six years before he was freed.

When we were done touring the castle, we conveniently hopped on a bus across the street, picked up our luggage, took the next bus to town where the train station was (the busses run every ten minutes like clockwork), and bought our train tickets just before hopping on the train, all in less than 30 minutes. That would have NEVER occurred in Italy.

I would like to compare transportation and getting around in general between countries. First I should mention Munich seemed to have a pretty good transportation system, but I must say that Switzerland cities have proven to be much easier and convenient to get from place to place, albeit we were visiting more modern, urban places in Switzerland as opposed to the places we visited in Italy this trip. Still, even comparing where we were to Florence and Venice (which I know is in its' own league), it seems the transportation system is more developed and user-friendly here in Switzerland. As a tourist trying to get around, especially with luggage, this is important. As charming and unique as Italy is (and how completely different from any place I have ever been), it can be frustrating when you "just want to get there already. (I really do understand the whole backpacking in Europe concept now though.) Italy does exceed Switzerland in how far your money goes however, as it is not nearly as expensive. Italy is a significantly larger country to explore with Central and Southern regions, in addition to the Northern, where we visited on this first trip. The nice thing about Europe as a whole is how easy it is to go from country to country, which is why we visited so many in one trip.

We are now on a speed train to Paris! We have been on regular trains, some with actual restaurant cars (not just fast food), a tilting train that tilts as it goes around curves, and now this one (which also has a restaurant car which I am about to hit up once I am done typing this entry).

I am looking forward to Paris. It is a place that is not new to Jeff unlike Austria, Italy, and Switzerland. He has been to Northern Germany about ten times (Munich only once before), and Paris approximately six or seven times. He will be my tour guide and it will be nice to not feel lost with him, but rather turn to him for his knowledge and direction. He has some spots he would like to show me and I am sure I will want to explore some new places for him as well. Hopefully, after leaving Paris, and sharing my insights with him, he will see Paris in a slightly new and different way than he did before.

It looks like we just entered the French border!

Okay, we just went to the restaurant, which on this train was more like a snack bar with alcoholic drinks included. I never before considered visiting Pakistan but here is what happened. We got beer and wine and some chips in the dining car and wanted to toast each other in French but didn't know the correct words to use. We asked a man standing there if he knew and went through the gamut of "cheers" in English, "salute" in Italian, "prost" in German, but then turned to him to ask if he spoke French. He did not, but knew English fairly well. He told us he was from Pakistan and was intrigued that I looked (90%, all but skin color) like a 'film artist" who is famous in Pakistan. We made friends with him. He took my picture with him – three times, each time changing the way he buttoned his shirt or fixed his hair and each time saying, "one more!". He then told us he might visit California next year and we invited him to email us and to let us know when so we could show him around. He told us he was a politician (so a VIP no less) in his country. When we told him all the places we have been and where we plan on going, he asked if Pakistan was on the list. We told him it hadn't been a consideration as of yet, but perhaps. He told us he would be our tour guide and when I asked if it was safe he said, "No problem." He explained that the media really paints a negative picture. I don't know what to believe but hey, with a politician maybe we would be pretty well taken care of!

After Arriving In **Paris**

When I stepped off that train and into the busy transport station it was overwhelming (but exciting too)! I have lived in big cities all my life, and for some reason due to the swarms of people and multitude of languages, nationalities, chaos, unfamiliarity and too many choices of where to go, I felt completely lost. However, it was okay because I had Jeff as my guide, right? So, we finally got sorted and got our unlimited metro, bus, and other access to public transportation passes.

Since I had never been to Paris before, I relied on Jeff to be the knowledgeable (Joe Cool) guide as we were amongst strangers riding on the metro. Instead and to my demise, the "Norbert" (as I call him at times like this), nerdy, disorganized side of Jeff came out as he ended up taking out his map and getting it caught in his black-rimmed reading glasses, whereby it had devoured his whole face. At this point the guy next to him starting chuckling, I looked the other way as if I didn't know him, and when he finally tried to put everything away, it looked as though he had dropped something important. When I asked what it was, his response was, "Oh never mind that, it was just a section of my map that ripped off as it got caught in my glasses." (I was rolling with laughter!) Jeff then asked, "Are you going to write about that?" (You betcha!)

It gets better! Our stop finally came and I had a moment of panic. We became dumb Americans once again with our ton of luggage about to miss our stop because we couldn't figure out how to open the door to get off. We got laughed at again by a nice young woman, who did also help us out.

We got out of the underground life (or in this case the metro, or subway as we know it in the states) and finally saw daylight. I am actually very fascinated and impressed with the transportation system here. I guess it makes sense to have such an elaborate system given all the swarms of human cattle all over the place. We checked into our hotel in Paris, which is an easy ¾ of a block from the metro (Go Jeff!). In Rick Steve's book, "Europe Through the Backdoor", (which I have been reading, has highly prepared me for this trip, and would recommend to any new Europe traveler), he spoke about how small hotel rooms are and how the bathrooms are usually airplane size. However, up until now that has not been the case. Now I know exactly what he meant.

11:40 pm Friday, July 29, 2011

We went out on the streets of Paris tonight and what can I say…Paris is FUN! I can now say, in comparison to all the other places on this trip, that none compete with the nightlife Paris has to offer. You get entertained everywhere you go – at dinner about 20 feet from our table was an older man, his band, and an older woman dancing to Dixie music. When walking around the city afterwards, there were endless shops, vendors, restaurants, bars and clubs. We saw a great juggler that had a goldfish bowl balanced on his head, performing for people right at their table. Even when we got on the metro, a young guy started playing classical music on the accordion.

Speaking of the metro, on our way out tonight, Jeff had another blunder as he stood up to get his map again. As he tried to re-locate his jump seat he missed it and nearly fell on his butt. I couldn't help but bust into laugher and the woman across from us could barely contain herself either.

Tomorrow is our last day and evening of this fabulous vacation (or "holiday" as Europeans call it). We are going to the Eiffel Tower first thing in the morning then viewing other sites.

7:20pm Saturday, July 30, 2011

We had a very full day with a lot of walking, even with the metro taking us within blocks of everywhere we want to go. We got to the Eiffel Tower around 9:30am and had a line that took almost an hour until we got into the first cable car. Once we reached the platform, the view was terrific but the elevator up (what seemed like another 50 plus stories) was what really took the cake. We went up to the rooftop, walked around the whole perimeter, and enjoyed the panoramic view. It gave me a true perspective of just how huge of a city Paris is. There were buildings as far as the eye could see. I have been up the Empire State building and, in comparing New York with Paris from that high up, it appears that Paris is a larger city. But upon researching the facts, greater Paris is only about a tenth the size of greater NYC, fascinating!

On our way down from the Eiffel Tower (which Jeff said was much more crowded than he had remembered), we decided to take the stairs from the platform level since the cable car lines were long and it was getting pretty breezy that high up. As we started our descent, after about ten flights of stairs, I started wondering if this was such a good idea. It seemed we weren't making any progress but there was no turning back now, since we would only have to climb up (which is even worse) in order to be back where we started. Eventually we hit ground level but now I know why people wait in the long lines.

Our next destination was near the area which I enjoyed the night before, which we learned is the Latin corner. We grabbed some delicious crepes and continued toward the <u>Memorial of Deportation</u>. This memorial was built in remembrance of those taken from their homes in World War II out of Paris and brought to concentration camps unknowingly with a 3% return rate. I read the sign when entering "silent please" and almost immediately lost it again. It was nothing like my experience at Dachau however.

From there we walked along one of the bridges and noticed hundreds of locks with ribbons and names of people on them attached to the railing. I had no idea what it symbolized. I figured it was a memorial of some sort, but when I asked someone the answer surprised me. We came to find out it was actually a symbol of everlasting love where couples write their names on the lock with the date and whatever else they wish, and throw the key into the <u>Siene River</u>. What a different and neat idea. On our mile walk toward the Louvre Museum, I purchased a lock and key so that later we could make our mark in Paris as well.

At the <u>Louvre</u> we saw the famous "Mona Lisa." I was surprised how small the painting was compared to enormous others that filled up entire walls, (even in the same room), and didn't get as much attention. After viewing Mona Lisa, we found our way to the famous "Venus de Milo" and it was funny because I had dropped my ticket somewhere and needed it again to view the gallery where that statue was located. All I could do was tell the attendant I lost it and hope they would let me in anyway. I reached the entrance and explained, "I lost my ticket visiting Mona Lisa but I am just here to see Venus de Milo and then we are leaving." They looked at me without knowing what to say but proceeded to let me in. It was as if I was trying to convince them that I was on a special guest list or something and the truth of the matter is, I couldn't even tell you who Venus de Milo is. *History is not one of my strengths admittedly, and nowadays, I could look up anything on google and have at least a basic answer to any, (no offense Venus de Milo).*

By this time I was completely exhausted and we got on the closest metro (just half a block from the museum luckily) and got back to our hotel for some downtime, which entailed a two hour nap.

Next update will be the last night in Paris!

Last Evening in Paris

Our last evening got off to a late start but that was what I wanted; to try to get my body started on the time adjustment that will be taking place again. We headed out around 10:30pm and when we got to the downtown area you would never know it was close to 11:00pm. The streets were packed! We first asked how late the restaurants were open because, although we weren't yet hungry, we didn't want to miss our last opportunity for a nice foreign meal. Not to worry, closing time was not until 1:00am! Gotta love Paris. It's like what they say about New York, "the city that never sleeps."

We walked around and saw a few street performers and I looked for some last minute souvenirs. We then had a nice dinner at a fondue restaurant with a patio great for people watching. (*It didn't compare to the fondue dinner we had in Luzern, Switzerland however*). After dinner we sat in a piano bar in the Latin corner area near where we ate, and listened while sipping on a drink.

After we left the restaurant and bar area, we strolled down by the river where we were earlier in the day and found a place to put our lock. On the lock we wrote, "Jeff + Stacy" on one side and the date (7-30-11) as well as a heart followed by "4 ever". Corny, I know but sweet, isn't it? We then threw the key in the Seine River. When I learned why they had all those locks earlier in the day, I just had to partake. We now have something special and sentimental to come back to in Paris one day.

Then came the rest of our evening. I asked Jeff earlier that afternoon about how late the metros ran and he convincingly told me that he was sure they ran all night. He even justified his answer by saying "it would probably cost them more to pull a train off the track then to keep them running." I accepted that answer and put it out of my mind. However, it was after 2:00am when we reached the metro to return to the hotel, and as we were about to enter the stairway down, a group of young adults came up and told us in French, (then one interpreted in English), that the metro is no longer running. We were definitely not in walking distance and, other than heading in the south direction, we would have no idea what bus to take. We were about to try to find a taxi when one of the guys in the group offered to escort us to the bus stop and guide us where to get off for our hotel. He and his two friends ended up taking the bus with us and we actually had a very enjoyable experience, so Jeff was off the hook this time.

We learned some interesting things about the "real" underground Paris that I would have never known if we hadn't run into these people. I was aware that below the subway level there is an elaborate sewage system that you can actually get tours of but he was talking about a level even below that! He, being about 20 years old, explained that it was a place where young people hung out and partied but that it could be dangerous in parts where the city is subject to caving in. The attraction apparently is that there are miles of tunnels and essentially caves under the city where you can't hear the city noise or see much light. Not exactly my idea of "getting away" but Jeff and I joked with our new friend that now that we know about this, we could save money on a hotel next visit. Anyway, it was an interesting fact that many tourists may never find out, or care to for that matter.

On the other hand, he did inform us about something that we could actually have benefited from if we only knew. He explained, if you see a ton of parked bikes unlocked, they are community bikes that anyone can pick up and ride, then drop off at another community bike parking area. I was so impressed with how a big city like Paris has that level of trust and sense of community to pull that off successfully. Nice work, Paris.

The Nightmare at the Paris Airport

I don't know if I would be willing to fly out of Paris again if I can help it. First of all, since Jeff and I were on two separate flights and different airlines (US Air for him and United for me), I needed to make sure I got my carry on from him before we split. I had three bags and he only had two, so he took some of the load off of me like a gentleman. However, we somehow got separated early and I panicked because we hadn't said goodbye yet and he still had my bag! Eventually we turned on our cell phones and texted our way back to one another, but by then we had just a second before he needed to get to his check-in area. Anyway, I got my bag but that is where the nightmare actually begins.

The check-in line was NOT moving and it was getting dangerously close to the time of boarding. I was accused of cutting in line, which, if I did, was not intentional and may have been done in my panic of trying to find Jeff before it was too late. Luckily a French-speaking traveler reassured me I was okay to stay in the line I was in. However, by the time I finally reached the kiosk to print my boarding passes, it was past the time the computer was able to print boarding passes. The departure time was about 30 minutes out and I had not checked my bags in or had a boarding pass in hand. Everyone, at this point, started wondering what was going on but the attendants didn't seem to want to give much information. I felt totally at their mercy (and I don't mean "merci" either).

Because this check-in process was so chaotic, eventually they had to notify the flight crew they needed more time to check passengers in and our flight was delayed due to their lack of efficiency and understaffing. This was only the precursor of the real nightmare however. I finally got to the check-in counter, had to pay an extra $70 for an extra bag and had no time to question it, and was given an urgent pass to get me through security quickly so that the plane didn't leave without me!

Although I was thankful for the kind gesture, it made me more nervous, almost like since they gave me this quick pass it would ultimately be my fault if I ended up missing the plane after all. In my state of anxiety and confusion, I sort of panicked again as I ran in the direction I thought I needed to go only to find a taped off area indicating that that ramp was closed. I felt so lost not knowing the language or being able to read or even interpret the signs, all the while knowing I may have only minutes left to make the flight to the states and missing it would mean I would be stranded here without Jeff.

By this point I felt desperate for some help. By the time I was nearly in tears, an overweight, pot-bellied, French airport staff man came to my rescue. I showed him my urgent pass and my boarding pass and he grabbed me by the arm and we ran throughout the airport together. I barely noticed as he was whispering, "I love you. I love you" in my ear. Anyway, he got me right through the security line in a jiffy and continued to escort me almost to the security area where my gate was now in sight. Although I was thankful for his help and basically done with him at that point, he proceeded to ask me if I would French kiss him! I immediately pulled away from him and said, "No!!" He then mumbled something to the extent of "ok" and finally let me go on my merry way. I couldn't believe what just occurred! This sort of thing would have never happened in the U.S., at least not that openly. I figured he knew he could get away with trying since I was in such a hurry that I didn't have time to file harassment charges or anything. Anyway, that was the real nightmare.

Upon Arrival to Chicago

My journey was half over at this point, eight hour flight followed by this four and a half hour layover then another four hour flight. However, since landing in America I felt like I was already home. Sometimes when you are far away from home, you just want to dissociate from your familiar ground and be where you are. However, once on familiar ground again, you transition to wanting to claim what's yours and feeling that sense of pride (which almost felt lost at least during those times when I felt like a "dumb American").

This became particularly evident to me when I entered customs. The separation between US Citizens from "Visitors" made me feel relieved that I was no longer a foreigner. I felt proud to be standing where I was. It was as though I had the upper hand now, although as I wrote earlier I do respect, now more than ever, what it feels like to be a true outsider trying to fit in (or at least just survive) in a foreign place. I must say that I do like the challenge at the same time, and will definitely take it all again. I love the adventure and am hungry for more. It does feel good to be "home" again though.

Lastly, I find it interesting, even within the United States, how people from different parts can be more diverse than people living in similar conditions half a world away. For example, if you grew up on a farm driving a tractor, raising chickens, having never rode a subway or learned how to navigate your way through crowds, you might be more similar to someone in a faraway Austrian village than to an

American New Yorker. In turn, the New Yorker may have much more in common with someone living in Paris than the American farmer. I never had this perspective before my trip to Europe.

Summary and Random Afterthoughts

I forgot to mention a game we played throughout Europe, and not to offend anyone, but I put the stereotype that Europeans don't shower or shave to the test. We started keeping track of how many offensive B.O.'s (body odors) we smelled that justified mention. To my surprise, (and relief!) it was nothing like people say. I will never take that stereotype seriously again. Anyway, for the whole two weeks I counted five times (no more than here in the states), until I got on the metro in Paris, where it went up to about eight to ten just during rush hour alone. If you can't tolerate this type of thing, time your traveling is all I can say.

As for the stereotype of the majority of women not shaving, no evidence of this whatsoever. Lastly, on this same note, I was more concerned about being able to tolerate heavy smoking everywhere we went and I suppose times are changing there too since the amount of people smoking in public places was actually no different, and maybe even less, than in the U.S.. I figured that would be one thing I would really struggle getting used to after living in California for so long (where there are strict laws about smoking in public), but it was no problem at all.

Best Meals and Memories

Germany – Meal with Mathias and Silke and their two sons at **Spatenhaus in Munich.**

The meal we had on the college campus.

Austria – The **Mozart Dinner Show** because of its uniqueness and beautiful setting and opportunity to meet people from all over the world sitting at your table.

The meal at the Malafrasca with our friends with the cold meat and cheese platter that we all shared.

Italy – The dinner in the Chianti region was excellent and had great ambience. The lunch we had in Siena where we were among the locals watching the car racing. I regret I didn't catch the names of these restaurants, but Italy has exceptional food everywhere you go so it is very difficult to go wrong.

Switzerland – Both restaurants were superb (the **Fondue Restaurant in Luzern**) and the one in **Montreux** called **Chateau** overlooking the lake which had great seafood.

Paris – More than the food, I found the people watching made it most memorable.

Most Memorable Fun Activities

Austria – Salt mines and Ice Caves
Italy – Getting lost in the **Venice** "maze" as I call it (after dumping off our luggage of course)
Switzerland – Mt. Palides and **tobogganing**
Paris – Nightlife and people watching

Besides this particular trip that Jeff and I took over a decade ago, I have not only learned so much about other countries and cultures, but about the whole concept of travel. Every time a two or three week vacation like this is over and we board the aircraft anticipating our 12-18 hour flight (depending on where we are in the world) back to the American West Coast, I feel bittersweet. I know I will miss the beautiful countries and nice people we met as well as just being so far away from our normal lives. The flip side is we do get to come back to our life and, fortunately, it is a pretty good one that we have created.

This is something I really want readers to understand. Vacations should not be all that you live for, even if they are one of the few things you save money for and may be the most exciting thing you do in your life. It is heathier to feel good about coming back home and sharing with your friends and loved ones the experiences you have had, than feeling dreadful that you had to leave. Remember that no matter where you have been fortunate enough to land, you always take a piece of that with you which adds to who you already were. Then, sharing your experience with others allows you to relive it again and again, and hopefully inspiring others to do the same

THE GIFTS OF TRAVEL

CHAPTER 4

ELEVEN WAYS TRAVEL FEEDS YOUR SOUL

Although we are blessed to have people enhance our lives whom we learn from daily, we also need to search inward to solidify meaning in what is taught. "Change Comes From Within" is the motto I printed (*before the digital world was more efficient*) on my business cards. I strongly believe in anything you can do to foster inner growth whether it be spiritually, learning new things, or experiencing new places. Without insight into what you are witnessing, you only see things at surface level, as if life is just passing through you. When you develop a "traveling mind", it enhances the way you process and commit your experiences to memory. If you allow your mind, no matter where you are in the world, to stop and internalize what you are experiencing in any given moment, you are no longer just a bystander, but an active participant. You will not only get much more meaning out of each new experience, but it will help cement those memories so that you can more easily access them whenever you want to bring them back to life.

For me, traveling is more than just a getaway or an escape. It has now become a passion that periodically longs to be fulfilled. Whether it be playing sports, painting, playing music, writing or reading books, if you do not feed your passion, you starve yourself of what is necessary to really feel alive. Once you get a taste for traveling and have had the experience of loving it with meaningful intention to grow as a person, it becomes very difficult to stop. I have heard many travelers I know say, "I feel like I am working now just to be able to travel".

Traveling can certainly be addicting, but one way to keep the positive vibe after traveling alive is to speak of it often. Let the effects of what you just experienced stay fresh by introducing it to someone who has not yet had the pleasure. If you feed the soul of another by spiking their curiosity, it can be fulfilling as well. This helps you get through the times in between travel experiences rather than just yearning for the next one. In other words, milk each memory for all it's worth and allow it to benefit not just you, but others around you.

Nowadays, people are finding ways to incorporate travel into how they work, such as working remotely. Some people chose to completely immerse themselves in another culture for an extended period of time and become expats. I believe change keeps you from being stagnant, which is why I love to travel to new places and meet new people. There are various ways to prevent one from having a mundane life, but I have found travel to be a wonderful and enlightening way to achieve this. Even when I am home, I can access my traveling mind and revisit those memories and apply them to my current life endlessly. Although some things are such that "you have to be there" to understand, I will do my best to share the feelings and thoughts I have at the start of any trip, particularly when flying somewhere.

From the moment I get on a plane and it lifts into the air, I take a deep breath and immediately smile at the thought of being "away". Away is what vacation is all about for me, not because I need an escape from life and people so much as I like to avoid "sameness". Think about what happens when you are consumed by routine and daily responsibilities without disruption. Are you constantly tied to endless unfinished business - phone calls, laundry, dirty dishes, having to be places, paying bills, worrying about bills not being paid, planning things, fixing things, being available for whatever comes up? You may be thinking, "is this all that life is"? My answer is, "no, never, it can always be more if you open the door and allow for a disruption". Disruption in a good way, of course. Disruption of the mundane, which allows you to grow and feel alive again.

For me personally, it is usually when I am far enough away, relaxed, and worry-free that my creativity and imagination is most accessible. This is when I do most of my writing. Obviously getting away is a necessary ingredient in order for me to write a travel book, but even other writings I am pursuing, like songwriting, seem to make the most progress when I am at a healthy distance from the daily routine. I strongly encourage everyone reading this to give yourself the gift of time, not just to others, but to yourself as well.

In this process of having deep conversations with interviewees introduced in Chapter 2, I noticed that experienced travelers have a certain way of approaching the world. My concept of the **"traveling mind"- the idea that you can grow internally much more deeply if you expand yourself externally**, is captured well in some of the quotes below. I have organized them into the following themes:

1. Traveling provides an education you cannot get at home or learn in a book or classroom.

"Traveling ignites passion for learning, provides self-exploration, and makes you let go of those boundaries. Travel is the only thing you buy that makes you richer."
Kathryn R. - Retired History Teacher and World Traveler

"Traveling opens you up to new experiences, new cultures, new ways of thinking and forces you to go inside and discover new things about yourself that you may not have been aware of."
Eric G. – Expat and Digital Nomad, World Traveler

"Traveling opens my eyes to the rest of the world and I believe that everyone needs to have an understanding of what else is happening besides our immediate span of influence."
Deneen Andrades – Life Coach, Public Speaker, Published Author, World Traveler

"Due to the pause of the world (referring to the pandemic) we have been mainly only able to travel within, and although some of the greatest journeys were taken with the least distance, now we can draw it back out into the world again."
Ian McCartor – Singer/Songwriter, Musician, Artist, Former Hospice Traveling Nurse, Retreat Planner

2. Traveling connects and bonds you with people you would otherwise never meet.

"It provides lifelong connections from all over the world! Each person comes from their own unique journey, and when we merge for a week.. the stories, the inspiration, the friendships formed - it's SO special and a passion of mine that I will never stop offering!"
Brittany Bamrick – Co-Founder of Bliss Camp Yoga Retreats

" Few things get me more excited than introducing friends that haven't met yet and seeing how that experience starts a new chain of people who were meant to be together. The castle is a symbol of human potential because we are all here to become something in life and to be surrounded by what once was an idea and is now a lasting piece of artistry."
Ian McCartor – Singer/Songwriter, Musician, Artist, Former Traveling Hospice Nurse, Retreat Planner

"It is not just about the group you are traveling with, but also meeting people from that location and observing what people in other cultures laugh at and find funny." Deneen Andrades – Life Coach, Public Speaker, Published Author, World Traveler

"I have found that in poor countries people are much friendlier and more giving."
Erin M. - World Traveler, Was an Expat in Several Locations

"You can go to a resort and still know nothing about the place after your visit, whereas living amongst the residents, you can get a better feel for the community and meet the locals. This way, we know how they eat, shit, shower, and shave."
Susan Tate – wife of Geoffe Tate (former singer for Queensryche) and originator for Back Stage Pass Travel, Extensive World Traveler (over 300 days a year)

Susan also elaborated on how quickly BSPT travelers bond when they never knew one another before. *"Every time we ask people their favorite part, it's always 'the sitting around and playing guitars'. When you travel with a group like this it forms lasting lifetime friendships. People, from these trips, are going to each other's weddings and houses. The first eight people in the original Italy group have stuck together on tours again and again. I feel honored to be a part of that. Traveling together bonds people."*

"Traveling has not just exposed me to more culture and food but also made me appreciate people, which is something that I didn't consider before. I didn't think I liked group travel until I started to travel with like-minded people that had common thread interests. For ex: Back Stage Pass Travel – fun group, gone repeatedly. It's opened me up to the possibility of things I would not have previously considered and I made friends."
Jeff C. – World Traveler and My Partner

"Travel truncates the time it takes to make friends with fellow travelers whom you previously didn't know. It can be more intimate than even knowing your own neighbor."
Saurabh Gupta, Ph.D. - Psychologist

"Some of my closest relationships are the friends I've met while traveling. Even though I have met some of these people only once, it's totally normal to reach out after a year or two of no contact and let them know you are visiting their country and meet up."
James K.- Pilot

3. Traveling With Others Deepens Existing Friendships

"Traveling with a few close friends reminds us why we became friends in the first place. It is so much more fun to check things on your bucket~ list alongside people who understand and cherish you. The magic is you are able to see your travel companions out of their daily element, in their vacation selves."
Kathryn R. - Retired History Teacher, World Traveler

"You learn a lot about a person when you travel with them and the learning process starts even before you leave from the way they pack."
Rachel Johnston -Self-Love Coach, Group Leader/Retreat Planner

"Because of the shared experiences, memories, and history, traveling gives you a reason to keep in touch because you can build from those memories and create new ones."
Deneen Andrades – Life Coach, Public Speaker, and Published Author

"As a result of traveling to the same places I have been before but now with my partner, I can see the same things in new ways by mutual sharing."
Ian McCartor – Singer/Songwriter, Musician, Artist, Former Traveling Hospice Nurse, Retreat Planner

4. Traveling allows you to see how universal the world is.

"You get to experience others' viewpoints and yet see we are all so similar."
Brittany Bamrick – Co-Founder of Bliss Camp Yoga Retreats

"What I get most out of traveling is meeting people and broadening my perspective by learning about both differences and commonality of people around the world."
Bobbi G.– Retired High School Teacher and Travel Agent, My Mother

"At the end of the day traveling has helped me see people as people. Over time it has helped me see we are all just here to live together and to love each other. Travel leads to compassion which is necessary for growth and peace. Without compassion there is judgement and judgement leads to conflict. I like the old saying, "walk a mile in another man's moccasin". What was so strange before becomes familiar and vice-versa. I enjoy the journey."
Ian McCartor – Singer/Songwriter, Musician, Artist, Former Traveling Hospice Nurse, Retreat Planner

5. Traveling forces you to be present and flexible.

"Traveling gives you permission to explore and experience places from a place of curiosity and wonder. You don't dwell on the past or think too far ahead in the future. Instead, you are present with your now-moment experience."
Kathryn R. – Retired History Teacher and World Traveler

"I ALWAYS love that first stroll in a new place (or a new neighborhood). The architecture, smells (if they are good), fashion of the people, different language snippets, and energy. I love the unpredictable factor about never really knowing what's going to be around the next corner."
Eric G. – Expat and Digital Nomad, World Traveler

"Sometimes being noncommittal is the best form of commitment because you are committing towards a high level of flexibility."
Jeff C. – World Traveler and My Partner

"Sometimes the unexpected brings some of the best experiences."
James K. – Pilot

"Traveling teaches you to be mindful about where you are going and to participate in the process."
Ian McCartor – Singer/Songwriter, Musician, Artist, Former Traveling Hospice Nurse, Retreat Planner

6. Traveling is good for your mental health and emotional well-being.

"Traveling promotes happiness, wonder, and surprise. It's a reminder that we all want to laugh, love, be with loved ones, enjoy good food, and listen to soothing music. It gives us a renewed sense of humanity by the time you get home."
Kathryn R. – Retired History Teacher, World Traveler

"I prefer depth instead of breadth, but the search is important because the breadth will show you where to invest the depth. You never know unless you go on the search."
Ian McCartor – Singer/songwriter, Musician, Artist, Former Traveling Hospice Nurse, Retreat Planner

Travel is both a luxury and a gift, even when you see things that are disquieting or bleak. Travelers should be ready to embrace the whole experience."
Saurabh Gupta, Ph.D. - Psychologist

7. Traveling gives you a new perspective on life and changes you.

"Even the "same places" aren't static over time. While places change and evolve, people also change and evolve seeing the "same place" with different eyes. Travel rejuvenates, invigorates and teaches patience. It forces you to surrender control to the uncontrollable, and when you effectively problem solve, you'll discover how resourceful you are."
Kathryn R. – Retired History Teacher and World Traveler

"It inherently makes you more flexible, more adventurous, more outgoing, more open-minded."

Eric G.– Expat and Digital Nomad, World Traveler

"Returning home from a trip to a developing nation or one in which economic oppression imposes heartbreaking difficulties on a population – such as Cuba – I find myself profoundly grateful for the opportunities the United States offers its citizens. Notwithstanding, it is critical to decentralize America when one travels, bearing in mind that the USA is not the center of the world, just part of the whole planet. Doing so keeps the mind receptive to the nourishment people find in other cultures where other values such as community and family are prioritized (far more than in America) name just a few."

Saurabh Gupta, Ph.D. – Psychologist

"When I travel, it's more of an experience than a trip. I immerse myself in the culture and read a lot before, then learn even more once there. Traveling allows you to see the world and get outside your bubble and comfort zone."

Erin M.- World Traveler, Was an Expat in Several Locations

8. Traveling to new places makes you more accepting and understanding toward others.

"Traveling to new places is what defines humanity. It may be what defines life itself. Sometimes, the beauty is less about aesthetics and more about that first conversation with a local. I am often pleasantly overwhelmed by their openness and rich culture. Travel teaches us to be tolerant and flexible. You will learn to appreciate people from all different walks of life."

Kathryn R.– Retired History Teacher and World Traveler

"My reasons for traveling are to open my eyes to culture, religion, poverty, and various lifestyles. As a result I have compassion, respect, and love for the people around this globe."

Mike L.– Extensive World Traveler

"Each trip has been a joy of discovery, a humbling experience about what the world has to offer, and a reminder how linked we all are, despite our differences. Hopefully traveling makes people more open to accepting the ways of others (whether while traveling or at home).
Steven B. and Laurie T.– Retired Forensic Psychologist/Retired Archeologist and World Travelers

"I'm interested in learning and paying close attention particularly to how other countries treat people who are not at the top of their financial ladder."
Deneen Andrades– Life Coach, Public Speaker, World Traveler

"I appreciate kindness and have found that the people with the least tend to help you the most."
Erin M.– World Traveler, Was an Expat in Different Countries

9. Traveling allows you opportunities to give to others.

"I wrote a song entitled, "Remember to Move" which is on a traveling album of songs inspired from my travel experiences. When I travel, I don't feel like a tourist, instead I meet people and come to give, not to take."
Ian McCartor – Singer/Songwriter, Musician, Artist, Former Traveling Hospice Nurse, Retreat-Planner

"When helping people from poor countries with medical issues, it's all about learning how to work with a team and be more flexible and problem solve together."
Debbie L. (Extensive World Traveler and Humanitarian/Doctor)

"I like to find a place where I can create a "container", which is a safe space to grow and express oneself providing safety and community."
Rachel Johnston– Self Love Coach, Group Leader/Retreat Planner

It isn't just opportunities to give to the less fortunate, as in Debbie's case, or healing past traumas, as in Rachel's example. It is also fostering and extending love and passion for traveling to friends and family (including younger generations) who otherwise would not take the step into the unknown as these last few quotes capture.

"It's so great to have introduced and passed down the love of traveling to my children."
Bobbi G. - Retried High School Teacher and Travel Agent, My Mother

"By taking them on these journeys, I am offering a window into the world for each one of them. Travel experiences are some of the greatest gifts you can give to a young person."
Ian McCartor – Singer/Songwriter, Musician, Artist, Former Traveling Hospice Nurse, Retreat Planner

"I have found that people who say 'this is a once in a lifetime trip' later after they experience traveling with us, get the bug and return. We just gave them the safe place because some people just otherwise won't go out of the country and I want to give them a chance. I also want to find a way to help people travel who can't afford it."
Susan Tate – wife of Geoffe Tate (former singer for Queensryche) and originator for Back Stage Pass Travel, Extensive World Traveler (over 300 days a year)

10. Traveling humbles you as you realize how much you don't know, not just about the world, but even yourself.

"I love the fact that it is impossible to see EVERYTHING on earth. Traveling gives you countless irreplaceable learnings that we can pay forward to others and, just like a reset button, it forces us to refocus on what really matters."
Kathryn R.– Retired History Teacher and World Traveler

"The more you know yourself, the more you can love yourself, and traveling helps unveil your undiscovered parts. Being out of the day to day routine forces you to bring out another side and allows others to bring out things in you that you may not have known were there."
Rachel Johnston – Self Love Coach and Group Leader/Retreat Planner

"Travel showcases the truly remarkable diversity of humanity, vis-à-vis politics, economic structures, culture, use of land, and cuisine. I am struck by how, in some ways, we Americans have, to a degree, forsaken family relationships, friendship ties and connection by virtue of the design of our living situations and workplaces.
Saurabh Gupta, Ph.D., Psychologist

"When we realize we don't have all the answers, it teaches us humility and compassion. When challenged with not wanting to yield, it teaches us to be open again. You don't have to go so far at all to travel within. You can travel with a single step. Do you travel to escape or do you travel to discover? With the latter, you come closer to yourself, whereas the former you are running from yourself. I think the leaving and coming back and leaving and coming back ultimately led me to make changes in life to become who I am today."
Ian McCartor – Singer/Songwriter, Musician, Artist, Former Traveling Hospice Nurse, Retreat Planner

11. Traveling provides the best stories and memories and is life changing.

"After returning home from our adventure, travel always saturates the two of us with the greatest and newest stories to tell; creating memories that literally last a lifetime."
Kathryn R. – Retired History Teacher and World Traveler

"We face challenges together, laugh a lot, and create unforgettable memories."
Steven B. and Laurie T. – Retired Forensic Psychologist/Retired Archeologist and World Travelers

"I went from a single man, a nomad with no specific intention or goal except for life experiences, to a family man who brings the family along to experience treasures to share with those closest to me."
Ian McCartor – Singer/Songwriter, Musician, Artist, Former Traveling Hospice Nurse, Retreat Planner

FIVE TYPES OF TRAVEL & HOW THEY EACH BENEFIT YOU

In this chapter I will emphasize how traveling has different meaning to different people depending on where they are with themselves. I came up with some general benefits that any kind of travel can offer listed here:

Giving yourself a break from a stressful job, unhealthy relationship, or unhealthy living environment.

Finding and/or becoming yourself again by freeing restraints on your life.

Expanding your mind by being open to learning new things about yourself and the world around you.

Making changes and improvements within yourself and your life that are everlasting with each travel experience.

I will now go into specific bonuses by organizing types of travel into the following categories:

Type 1 - Solo

Although I personally have never done it to any great extent, there are many people who love to travel and explore on their own. People who prefer this type of travel are usually very independent, enjoy their own company, often are single or in a non-committed relationships, but sometimes just have a partner who does not share their interest in traveling.

Reported benefits are: being able to do whatever you want, whenever you want; not needing to consider anyone else's preferences or time constraints; having solitude to hear your own thoughts and be fully present with yourself; allowing yourself space to contemplate both mundane and serious life matters; learning how to enjoy your own company and how to feel complete even by yourself; relying solely on yourself to problem solve and trusting your own instincts; being free to be 100% yourself with no one there to judge you.

Type 2 - Couples

When it comes to traveling as a couple, having enough in common is important. Liking similar activities and food preferences, for example, makes the experience more bonding and enjoyable. There is usually more of a romantic focus on couples trips versus traveling with families or bigger groups.

An interesting thing to consider with newer couples is the fact that traveling together can either make or break the relationship. Therefore, it could be a good test to see if two people are, in fact, compatible since taking a trip brings new challenges and decision making junctures that can bring up stress. Travel can introduce traits and behaviors in one or both people that may not otherwise be recognized so soon in the relationship.

I have a few memories of traveling with new partners in my single years where by the third day, I could not wait to get home to have my space. Luckily, now I have a partner who I cannot wait to go away with and with whom I rarely get homesick when on a trip together. I suppose he passed the travel test many times over.

Type 3 - Family

These trips can be very bonding and special memory builders especially if there is open and non-judgmental communication among family members and they generally "like" each other, (but there are plenty of instances where this is not always the case). For those with young children, there is a big difference in the type of vacation it ends up being. When children reach an age where they can appreciate different cultures and countries, it is quite a gift to give them those opportunities.

For those fortunate enough to have close relationships with family and extended family, make the most of the time together, work out differences, and cherish the memories. For others who find it too difficult to spend extended time with family or do not have close relations, there are other ways to enjoy traveling with others who are not "technically" family.

Type 4 - Casual Group Travel with Close Friends

Many believe that blood is thicker than water, whereas others consider the quality of the relationship itself. No matter who they are or how you came to know them, it is important to balance time with people you love, whether they are family or the closest thing to it.

I have had wonderful experiences planning get togethers' and weekend getaways with couples or sometimes just my girlfriends. It's nice to have people in your life you are not embarrassed to share a room, or even a bed, with when the circumstances call for it. If you are blessed with the kind of friends who, no matter where you end up, it's always a good time just because of the company you are with, consider it a blessing.

These type of trips can foster deeper friendships and often times turn into more organized group trips over time. One example is a bunch of guys going away for a weekend, (a reunion of old friends going golfing), and years later becomes an annual event with t-shirts and all. For my neighbor Mike, of whom I am speaking, this year will be their 20th anniversary in which they attended a different location all over the United States. Another example would be casual camping trips that turn into annual Frisbee Golf tournaments 30 years later, as the TACI example I referenced prior and will expand more on later.

Type 5 - Organized Group Travel

Group travel has many components that differ significantly from all other forms of travel. It has a leader or group of leaders, and fellow travelers could be people you may or may not know well, or even at all. Group activities are organized to some extent. There are some rules, even if loose ones, to keep some sort of system or flow to the experience, which helps to avoid it getting out of hand or falling apart. (Of course with youth travel groups rules are much more important to specify.) Group travel also has many components of bonding and getting to know each other giving it that cohesive and "family like" vibe. One indication of a successful group travel experience is when people express sadness when it's over, exchange contact information, and keep in touch for months or even years later, all because of the group experience that was first created.

Besides the fond memories from summer camp and Israel that I shared about earlier, more recently, (but still in the last decade), I have gained many circles of friends through group travel, and it grows with every new experience. These relationships continue to deepen and get richer with each interaction building on the previous one. As others interviewed have also suggested, the quality of visits seem different with friends that you originally met while traveling than otherwise.

Once you decide on organizing group travel, a certain level of foresight, planning, and anticipation comes into play, so it is not something that gets thrown together last minute as it sometimes is with casual travel. One aspect worth mentioning is the balance between alone, couples, and group time. I love people and the closeness in my personal relationships. At the same time, I equally love my alone time and thoroughly enjoy my own company. (*If that weren't true, I would not be motivated to spend endless hours alone contemplating and writing the pages of the book you are now reading!*) I conclude it's best to have a healthy balance of space for self-reflection coupled with activities that fellow travelers share together. Group travel can offer everything that solo travel can (if it incorporates enough alone time) plus the added benefits of:

a.   Gaining clarity through sharing ideas with others
b.   Building trust
c.   Building new foundations for lifelong friendships

Because gaining trust and enjoying the company you have during travel experiences are so important, choosing the right travel partners to make the trip a success is key. I will go in depth in the next section of this book about healthy versus unhealthy relationships and how to choose your friends, plus many other relationship-oriented topics that are relevant to group travel. But first, I will show you that there is a group travel option for just about anyone and will expose you to a handful of my own personal examples of unique and life changing group experiences.

CHAPTER 6

THE VARIETY IN GROUP TRAVEL OPTIONS

The travel groups I have participated in range from very primitive to luxurious, sequenced in that order, and each had a theme of some sort which bonded fellow travelers. I personally know the founders of each because either I have known them prior to their launching of these ongoing travel groups, or I had the pleasure of getting to know them through the group travel experience (it's actually half and half). They have been among the interviewees introduced a few chapters ago, but now I would like to expand on how the actual group experience impacted me.

TACI

This, so far, has been a primitive, rather low key, come as you are, camping gear and bare necessities kind of trip. We usually all pitch in and bring food to share as well as making original drinks with a competition for the best one. The day time activities center around a frisbee golf tournament where we combine hiking with selecting trees, rock formations, or sign posts as designated targets in the course we spontaneously create. Most of the time we find nice campgrounds that are equipped for group camping (with both tent or RV options).

Last time the forest fire warning was high and did not allow firepits. Of course this was the last thing any of us expected, but we made the best of it. This was an example of "it's the people you are with" that makes the trip. A good group leader, such as my friend Erin, knows not just how to pick decent places, but has a talent for putting a compatible mix of people together. This was shown by how we all bonded in the cold evening with no fire to warm us up, yet kept each other entertained until we just wanted to curl up in our warm sleeping bags.

I asked Erin to give some background on how TACI was born. She explained "it started in law school with a group of friends who all liked nature and camping. We started planning backpacking and camping group trips and the same group would attend every year." I asked about the acronym and name origin and Erin explained that it was first called, "Tour All of California Independence Day". Over the years, conflicts with the Fourth of July for political or timing reasons came about and it was no longer consistently held on the holiday weekend. However, what was consistent was that it always included large amounts of alcohol consumption and was therefore renamed, "Tour All of California Intoxicated."

For many years, TACI was the only time this group of people saw each other. There was a "no kids" policy until one friend had a kid and suddenly that became null and void. Since then, these children have now grown up with TACI. As a result, Erin wants to change the name because she sees it has evolved into a solid group of friends just wanting to have good wholesome fun for the entire family with other yard games as well. She takes great pride with her creative side and enjoys decking out the campground with a fun and inviting flair. The main theme still centers around the Frisbee Golf Tournament. When asked how that became the theme, I expected a different answer, but got "I stole it from someone else". Erin does however put a lot of thought and originality into this annual event, and even makes her own trophies.

I am so happy and honored to be included in this annual camping event and look forward to it every year. My children are now a part of it and I am sure it will keep growing. Since it is not quite a public event, I will refrain from posting contact details for this particular one, but I will provide information about a few of the others, including the group travel community I am building!

Back Stage Pass Travel (BSPT)

These are quarterly opportunities (and are becoming even more frequent) to travel with Geoff Tate (the former singer of the rock band Queensryche and now for his current band, Operation Mindcrime). Seven day adventures to various places around the world ending on the last night with a back stage pass for his concert is what, Susan Tate (Geoff's wife) has created. It is a very unique experience with anywhere from 12-21 (depending on which trip) die-hard fans of Geoff Tate travel, eat, and sight-see together while living in fairly close quarters. (*We do get our own rooms and bathrooms in most cases, which could be a game changer for some, including me.*)

One of the best memories I have is in Germany with the wagon ride competition. We were broken into two groups, each with a musician from the band, singing random songs louder than the opposing wagon amongst the grape vines at the family-owned winery in which we stayed. It was a blast! Another great memory was in Tuscany where one evening I shared with the group an original song I wrote for Jeff to be sung at our wedding ceremony. I had never performed that particular song in front of an audience before (*of course Jeff had to isolate in our room during that time*). I appreciated the great support I received from this loving group of people.

Although we do have a rough itinerary going into each week-long trip, you must be flexible and accept Susan's tough love approach to things.

In other words, if you are not on the bus at the time she sets the night before, you get left behind! I would not describe these experiences as "relaxing", but rather "busy" full day itineraries that involve socializing, sight-seeing, learning, playing, laughter, drinking good wine, eating good food, and listening to outstanding music. You feel exhausted by the end of the day but are rearing to get up and do it all over again, and each day brings new pleasant surprises. It does get some getting used to but after signing up for 4 trips now, we have decided that it is well worth it, and we are careful to never miss the bus!

We have made some great friends in a very short time through of Back Stage Pass Travel and we have even invited some to our wedding. The goodbyes are always difficult as you feel a sense of "family" after spending day in and day out with others in such an intimate setting. As with all of these trips, there is a group chat created typically on WhatsApp and, after the Back Stage Pass trips, these group chats still continue on a daily basis. Travel members will go to their concerts when they show up to play in their home towns, so the bonding experience extends beyond the trip itself.

These are open to the public but I will forewarn you, once posted, they sell out literally in minutes or days. So check out the upcoming travel opportunities and decide quickly at **Backstagepasstravel.com.**

The Castle Retreats

We have been attending Ian McCartor's retreats in France for a number of years and he always brings unity amongst his friends from all over the world. They definitely have a spiritual vibe and always include original music. I have been inspired every time to write new songs where I can also run them by my trusted castle friends for feedback and support. Not to mention, the meals are all included as we sit family style each night for gourmet cooking crafted by Ian's mother Kim McCartor. She is a superb chef with a catering business called **Redbasket Catering**. She and her entourage of talented chefs concoct unforgettable dishes throughout the week.

Another highlight about these trips are the exclusive wine tastings we do at a mansion owned by Christophe, the owner of the castle and a few others in the area. He has an enormous collection of thousands of untouchable wines in his basement cellar rooms. There is an elaborate system for keeping each varietal at an exact temperature and in pristine condition. You really have to be there to believe it.

We truly feel like royalty at the Castle Retreats. It is luxury mixed with the nicest, most accepting people you will ever meet. Each year we have had the pleasure of seeing repeat guests as well as meeting new ones, so our friendship circle is constantly growing here as well with lifelong friends. With this group too, there are opportunities to see one another away from the castle as Ian or I or any one of us may plan additional local events. Ian has also held a pseudo-castle retreat in a unique dome-shaped rental home in California which brought similar calmness, music, and laughter the way the castle does.

At this point, Ian has a invite-only policy for the castle retreats in France, however as my group travel business develops, I am sure Ian, Kim (the chef), and I will be working closely to create some public opportunities so please stay posted by following **IanMcCartor.com** and/or my contact information at the end of this book.

Bliss Camp Yoga Retreats

Bliss Camp Yoga Retreats offers an interesting mix of challenging and uniting yoga classes with a variety of inspirational music from different genres. In addition, they take you on some incredible excursions and you stay in beautiful, luxurious resorts around the world. It was truly "blissful" from start to finish and had all the elements I love about a group experience with very accommodating and loving hosts, Brittany and Ashley.

My daughter Rachel originally knew about Bliss Camp and invited me to accompany her. After the retreat, we were asked to evaluate our experience and write reviews if we felt inclined to do so. I did and to my surprise many months later, while looking on their website to consider a future Bali retreat, I noticed my testimonial was published! I want to share it with you:

> *"I thought Bliss Camp was a wonderful experience. The people were all so kind and welcoming and it felt like family from day one. I felt the sincerity in our group leaders and it made our experience so meaningful. I would highly recommend doing this with or without a partner or friend as you will make new friends, but it was very special to share this experience with my daughter."*
> — STACY J.

Brittany created an environment for bonding with others as well as self-growth. This trip was so inspiring to me. She encouraged us to journal throughout the week and sharing this with you will give you a fuller flavor of my experience:

Sunday, Oct. 2nd, 2022

Life is really interesting, as I sit here in **Tulum, Mexico** (an absolutely beautiful place) at the Ayala Resort. Rachel invited me to go and she opened my eyes to so many new things and new perspectives. I probably wouldn't be journaling right now if it wasn't for her. Right now, she is getting a facial and I am sitting on the beach feeling the warm breeze and listening to the waves crash. We are at the yoga retreat and there are 30 wonderful people here with us. This morning was the best yoga class I ever had combined with great meditation as well as dance music. It was challenging, interactive, and a great work-out. After the yoga class we went on a Cenote tour and swam in these magical caverns and caves. I learned so much today. I learned the difference between a cavern (with openings for sunlight to come in) and a cave (completely dark). We got to swim in both and had waterproof flashlights. There were small crevices where we had to lay very low so as not to hit our head. It was quite the experience!

I also learned that knees hold our egos and when we bring our heart close to our knees we nurture that ego we love. Brittany also taught me that yoga is just a series of adjustments, and when you are uncomfortable, finding the solution is the key to living a better life. I feel whole and complete just sitting here by myself at the moment. As soon as my mango margarita arrives, I will join the group of new friends sitting by the water. It's been a great day!

(Later that same day) We just completed a meditation and were asked to journal our free flowing thoughts or to write about what we are grateful for. As always, I am grateful to be me. I am grateful for being here right now. I am grateful for the love I have to give. I am grateful for the love I receive. I am grateful for music, for the sound of laughter, for the warm breeze, for the sounds of the waves, and the birds. I am grateful for my father, for teaching me, for loving me, for being the wonderful person he was. I am grateful for my mother for being happy and for always wanting what she feels is best for me. I am grateful for my beautiful children – inside and out, and for believing in themselves and finding their way in the world. And I am grateful for Jeff for staying by my side through the years and letting me be me.

Monday, October 3rd, 2022

Today I made a commitment and invested in myself to take a coaching class on how to write and publish a book in 90 days. (*I was not being strict with that time-table by the way*). I want to write a book on the power of group travel. I am excited to start the program and since I will be actually traveling this month, it's a perfect time to start it! Yay me!

Wednesday, October 5th, 2022

Today is the last full day in Tulum. We leave tomorrow. Although it has been a soulful and memorable experience, I will be ready to return home tomorrow. However, Jeff and I leave for Amsterdam the next day for yet, another adventure! I expect that trip will be different than this one because the dynamics will be different. I will be more in charge of planning how the day unfolds. It will be more of a sightseeing/exploration trip vs. pure relaxation and soul-searching. However, after this experience, it has prompted me to work on always being present and open to soul-searching wherever I am and whomever I am with. If not, I may miss something important that the world and life have to teach me! That is probably the most impactful take-away I received from Bliss Camp and it is incredibly powerful. But here is a list of other things I have learned, or am continuing to learn, or was reminded of from this incredible retreat:

- You need to feel in order to heal (sometimes physically, but almost always mentally)
- The more you pay attention to something, the more energy you give it (both for good and bad) so you should choose your focus and intention carefully.
- I want to keep learning "myself" and teaching myself what I am capable of, then always strive to live up to my highest potential.
- I want to share with people who are at least willing and open to understanding me without judgement.
- I want to choose activities that not only heal me, but heal others. I also need to recognize that some activities may not always be shared experiences because everyone is different and unique and sometimes to heal someone else, you need to "do" very little.
- I also want to do whatever I can that is healing with my music/songwriting and want to find places where that is welcomed and desired.

Thanks to both Brittany and Ashley. I have become richer with all the gifts from the retreat experience they created. I encourage you to inquire about what they have to offer so I included their contact information below.

ashley + brittany // co-founders
instagram // @blisscampretreats

SECTION III

PSYCHOLOGICAL BARRIERS TO OVERCOME: HOW TRAVEL CAN BE THERAPEUTIC

The main purpose of this section is to show people how group travel and travel in general expands your perspective on the world. To do this, we cannot start globally, but rather individually. The next chapter will teach you how to wander within yourself and develop your traveling mind. Ensuring that our brains are functioning at their optimal level is important before we can appropriately take on bigger challenges.

In the beginning of this book I started off by explaining the importance of being human first. We are all imperfect and will continuously have things to learn and changes to make to better ourselves. Only once we have done the inner work, can we expect to have healthy relationships with others. In the next chapter I will explain what "inner work" means and how I have helped hundreds of people with this first step. The barriers that prevent healthy relationships from developing start with you. The next step would be connecting with positive influences in order to build long-lasting healthy relationships. Lastly, I will emphasize the importance of relying on these relationship skills to overcome your fears and get out of your comfort zone by exploring the unknown. Navigating the global world with your deeper inner self is what I found to be life changing.

In my experience of traveling with others to various places in the world, (and believe me I have been to some of the most unforgettable places!), I will reiterate that who you travel with can be just as, or maybe even more important, than where you travel to. That is why I took so much space in this book to unpack my thoughts and analyze what makes a healthy relationship. This, in turn, will help you make the best decisions about who you allow to get closest to you and why.

Whether you are primarily reading this book for traveling purposes, to learn about yourself, or for general curiosity, you will benefit from reading about how to maximize the amount of positive people in your life. I will discuss how to set standards for yourself, as well as boundaries with others who may not be serving you well. Then I will tie these ideas into how it can benefit you in everyday life as well as suggesting how traveling can expand your self-growth even further. Being this is the "self-help" section of the book, I have included some writing exercises (*thought provoking questions to answer and journal about*) throughout these chapters. Feel free to write in the book or print out the appropriate pages to fill out, as writing often has a different, more meaningful effect than just thinking about something in your head.

CHAPTER 7

LEARNING HOW (AND THAT IT'S OK!) TO PUT YOURSELF FIRST

How to Love Yourself By Becoming Your Own Best Friend

How we feel about ourselves will reflect how we relate to others. It is important to consistently love yourself even during times where we feel un-loveable (*and we have all been there*). For some, it is difficult to give self-love, simply (but also complexly) because we do not know how to love ourselves. Let's discuss why loving yourself can be such a difficult thing to do in the first place.

When clients say they don't deserve to be loved, it stems from somewhere. They tend to beat themselves up consciously and subconsciously because they were given the message that they aren't worthy or good enough at some point in their life. Although this is an awful way to think about oneself, some do not take responsibility for this self-sabotaging belief and instead blame their parents or caretakers. It is important to look into yourself, rather than blaming others, for not giving you what you know you deserve. We can change the way we feel and think if we want to. As a child we do not have all the resources to do that, but as adults we do.

As a child, we need and crave attention, validation, encouragement, and praise from others because we don't know how to give those things to ourselves. As an adult it is important to practice these skills. The better you get at giving to yourself, the less self-loathing behavior (in the form of anger, resentment, and blame) will take place. The danger of not learning to take care of your own emotional needs is that it causes harm in all the relationships in your life, whether it be your parents, friends, coworkers, lovers, spouses, or even your own children.

To avoid self-hatred, practice self-affirmations. You may struggle to come up with anything good to say as you look in the mirror, but everybody has some redeeming qualities, even in their darkest hours. Dig deep, acknowledge them, and with time and changes in your behavior and attitude, more good traits will come to the forefront. You are the biggest obstacle that is holding you back from being your best. Out of self-respect, I encourage you to give yourself that gift.

<u>Writing Exercise:</u>

What are three things you like or love about yourself that you can fall back on even when you are not feeling particularly proud or confident?

1. ____

   ____

   ____

2. ____

   ____

   ____

3. ____

____

____

Try to think of some things that only you, and no one else, can give you. It is much healthier once you realize you don't NEED anyone to survive other than yourself. Of course, it is always a blessing to have good people in your life, but at the end of the day, you know yourself best. You need to be your own best friend because nobody else will take better care of you and attend to your needs more readily and completely. Finding the space to be with yourself is essential and when you are in the grind of daily life, this may be hard to come by.

<u>Writing Exercise:</u>

What do you seem to rely on yourself for more than you rely on others to do for you?

____

____

____

Getting out of your zone and taking a trip is one of the greatest gifts you can give yourself. Even when traveling with others, it's important to take some alone time to reflect on who you are, what you love about yourself, and what you need to change. Once determined, you must support yourself in making those changes if it is going to materialize. Do you forgive your best friend for making mistakes? Assuming the answer is yes, then you should forgive yourself as well. That is what you do when you love another person. The next section will discuss how to love yourself.

How to Show Self-Love

Showing self-love means paying attention to what your body is telling you physically and emotionally. If you feel hungry, feed yourself. If you feel lazy and need motivation, exercise and move your body to get energy. If you feel tired at the end of the day, relax or close your eyes and take a power nap. Self-love is also listening to your heart. If you feel you want a hug from someone, ask for it. If you need to cry, allow yourself that privacy and space to do so. If you feel joy, allow yourself to express it in any way you want. If you want to be silly, allow yourself to be goofy and not care what others think. Whether it is a friendship or a romantic relationship, if you know being around a particular person is not healthy for your well-being, self- love is letting go.

Forgiving yourself for your mistakes is an act of self-love, but so is holding yourself accountable for your mistakes so you can improve. Loving yourself is accepting who you are, with all your faults and imperfections, as well as allowing your confidence to shine in the things you know you are good at. Don't listen when others say it is selfish to put yourself first and set boundaries if that is what you need. Instead of "self-ish", use the term "self-care". It is a more fitting description and does not have the negative connotation that is so unfair to put on yourself. Of course it is fine to help other people, but know if you are depleted, you are even more limited in what you can give to anyone else. To summarize, self-love is taking care of you first, and becoming the best version for you and those you love. Always remind yourself that you are worth your time.

<u>Writing Exercise:</u>

What are things you need in order to be stable, to feel whole, and to have before offering help to others?

____

____

____

Giving yourself the gift of travel is a great option that fills your cup because years after that trip has passed, you still keep the memories for a lifetime. When we get older, we lose our memory, it's true, but it's typically the short term that goes first (like not remembering where you left your keys or what you ate for breakfast). If you were to ask an older person about their childhood memories, they will most likely give you story after story, and sometimes flavored with astonishing and colorful detail. When I read my memoirs from traveling ten years ago, it gives me great joy and brings me right back to where I was at that time. It is a true gift and one of the best ways I know to show self-love.

Self-Commitment

Part of loving yourself is being strongly committed to your own growth and well-being. Committing to yourself means taking ownership of your behaviors, responsibility for your mistakes, and being the biggest cheerleader for yourself when it comes to your accomplishments. Understand the difference between "challenging" versus "scary" when trying new things. Push yourself enough to grow, but not overwhelm. Stop the "all or nothing" thinking. Speak with confidence and believe in what you say you are going to do and find just the right balance of how hard to push yourself. Always have your own back with the best intentions so you can reach your full potential. Forgive yourself when you fall short, pick yourself up when you fall, period.

When you deeply care for someone, you want to encourage them, you want the best for them, and you hurt when they hurt so therefore (*if they ask*) you want to give them the best advice you can, right? There is a commitment to always be there when they need you as a loyal friend. This loyalty should apply towards yourself as well.

This theme is relevant to traveling in that planning, agreeing to take time away from other obligations, and spending money is a true commitment. If you are traveling in a group, the commitment expands beyond yourself and includes commitment to your travel partners. With that comes trust, so trust in your ability to follow through with your commitments to both yourself and others.

<u>Writing Exercise:</u>

I challenge you to make a list of things you want to happen in your life and come up with a plan to execute them. It will do you wonders to check items off your list while proving you can trust yourself with your own commitments.

____

____

____

Situational Depression

There are times when we feel stuck and unable to follow through with our goals and commitments. It happens to everyone. We cannot go through life having never felt debilitating pain or confusion that stops us in our tracks at one point or another. We have and will continue to face difficult challenges because it is evitable. Many people are crippled by their past and burdened by regrets and self-blame. Staying in the past too long can lead to full-blown, clinical depression. On the other hand, thinking about and planning for the future can also be can be immobilizing, if you are too obsessive about the details. Staying in the future too much can caused anxiety. Depression and anxiety often go hand in hand. To have the right balance in life, it is necessary to use the past and future as a temporary tools, while mostly staying present as you progress on life's journey.

When there is no biological or hereditary component linked to a person presenting with depressive symptoms and a tragic circumstance has just occurred, we call it "situational" as opposed to "clinical" depression. Luckily it is temporary and lessens as the situation that prompted the depression improves.

Although some go straight to medication to resolve these feelings, the best way I see out of situational depression is to look for alternatives. Alternatives lead to hope. Hope leads to motivation. Motivation leads to change. The opposite (*doing nothing*) leads to complacency and hopelessness, which can turn very dark. Once you set foot on that dark path, it can be difficult to get off, and the further you walk down it, the gloomier it gets.

If you don't like the path you're on, try an offshoot. Take a new direction that you are unfamiliar with and see where that leads. Chances are any other road would be a better choice. Do it before it's too late to turn back. If you are reading this right now and this is resonating with you, it's not too late!

<u>Writing Exercise:</u>

What is the next path you are willing to take?

____

____

____

Stopping Unhealthy Cycles

Speaking of changing paths (especially if it involves another person), you have more power than you think. Sometimes you need to put your foot down once and for all, but remember, if you give someone an ultimatum you really need to mean it. If you chose to stay with someone even after telling them there is a condition that first needs to happen and they don't follow through, you will not be taken seriously. If you continuously don't keep your word whether it is to them or to yourself, people will lose respect for you very quickly. Many I have worked with find difficulty in doing what they know is best for them because they are so focused on pleasing others. A common scenario in this group is a longing, stemming from childhood, to get their parents approval because they were either told or made to feel they were never good enough. This foundation often leads to low self-esteem and people-pleasing behavior patterns that transfer into adulthood, creating an unhealthy imbalance of power in their adult relationships.

If you are not leading yourself, someone else can easily take the lead and it may not be to your benefit or the direction you want your life to go. Think of relationships as a dance. If you lead by changing the steps, it is no longer the same dance. Your partner will then have to make the adjustment or it doesn't flow, and sometimes it never will once those changes are made. In other words, changing unhealthy cycles with others needs to start with changing yourself. When it comes to your well-being, become the leader, not the follower, and make necessary adjustments that work for you. It may change your whole life trajectory for the better.

Getting away from an unhealthy situation by traveling can be an escape, but may only be temporary. Real change comes from changing within, not just your outer environment. However, if you use tools when traveling such as journaling, spending time to reflect, and getting new perspectives from having that needed distance, it can open your eyes and become more than a temporary band-aid approach.

<u>Writing Exercise:</u>

What steps can you make that would (*or could*) necessitate positive change in yourself, and possibly in someone close to you?

____

____

____

Don't Be a People Pleaser

People pleasers tend to feel responsible for others emotions. They feel that if they don't step up and help, nobody else will. That's simply not true. What did these people do before you were in their life for all those years? Also, will they be able to function if something unexpected were to happen to you and you were no longer available? Be careful not to create relationships where people depend on you too much. It could end up hurting them more than helping them in the long run. When people depend on you or others too much, they stop taking care of themselves. Alternatively, remember (*as discussed before*) you need to always make sure your tank is full before you offer to help others.

Be careful about developing patterns with people where, because you are too available, they automatically expect things from you that you can't fulfill. It can run you to the ground if you let it get too far where you end up having nothing left to give (such as time, energy, money). Setting boundaries is essential for your mental health, optimal functioning, time management, and balance in life. If you take yourself for granted, so will others, and you will have nothing for yourself.

I have spoken with people who say they want nice things, but always seem to deny their own needs, or feel they don't deserve it. Instead, they replace their own needs with satisfying others and eventually either give up their own dreams or wait too long and miss the opportunity. It's very sad to see this happen. Remember that life is short so do not neglect yourself. Be kind to others, yes, but not at the expense of your own happiness.

<u>Writing Exercise:</u>

What have you been giving up for others that you feel is holding you back from living your own life the way you really want to live?

____

____

____

Getting Your Life Back

Sometimes when we are stuck, we refuse to see a way out because we don't want to shatter our image of what we wanted, or of what others wanted for us. In order to heal from any situation, albeit a relationship or job, you need to face your truth and listen to your own thoughts instead of taking on those of others. If you know you are not happy, don't let others convince you otherwise. Your life is no one else's to decide, it's yours and you need to own it! Stay strong and be true to yourself. It's time to live your life the way you want to live it.

Sometimes it makes sense to explore things outside of ourselves to find what is within. That is one of the most amazing things I have found in traveling. The more you travel, the more the world shrinks, and the more you grow. It sort of puts your worries into perspective too, whereby familiar problems do not seem to takeover when in an unfamiliar environment. Even a small distance can make a big difference in giving you a new perspective. When good opportunities present themselves, take them!

What Money Can't Buy

The biggest take away I want you to get from this essay is that being happy may not mean having all the material things you ever wanted in life. Rather, what makes people most "internally" happy is loving who they are or are becoming. Money is a necessity, but it has its limits, and can only get you so far. It is a means to an end, and yet you can't take it with you in the end. Money is simply a tangible item with a number value that is only meaningful until it's gone.

In comparison, the most valuable things in life are things you may never physically touch. There is no numeric value to them because they are priceless, and they have everlasting meaning even beyond the time they exist. When it comes to spending money, you need to be smart and evaluate what you get in return for giving up the security of having it. However, the money itself does not matter, but since it's a limited resource, we need to think about what is worth spending that resource on. Interestingly, the highlights in most people's lives are those very things money can't buy.

The things that are most sacred and irreplaceable (which in my mind, equals "valuable") are things we most remember and that others will always remember about us. They are passion, friendship, laughter, and love. For me personally, all these precious gifts are "present" (*no pun intended*) whenever I travel (and yes at other times too). When looking back on all the money I spent on traveling, I do not regret a single penny because even the not so good experiences have me taught valuable life lessons that could only be learned by having been somewhere else. Again, priceless.

Most of us do not have disposable income, which is why I like to encourage you to do what is possible and to create the life you want for yourself, whatever that means. If you need to go small, go small but find a way to make the small BIG. I know people with little money who have a *wealth* of happiness because they know and have what matters to them.

<u>Writing Exercise:</u>

What things in life do you find most valuable and irreplaceable?

My Ideal Version of Happiness

This is a rather personal essay, specific for me, but I wanted to share it so you all can think about how you may tailor it to you. My ideal version of happiness is to not want for more. To be satisfied that if I died in this very moment that there would be a feeling of contentment with where I am in life, how far I have come, and how I've made amends with people I needed to. I would never want those I deeply love to ever doubt my feelings for them, and I wish to look back on my life with a sense of accomplishment and satisfaction with how I handled adversity.

My ideal version of happiness is to not have unfinished business and to feel a sense of closure on things that didn't make sense by creating my own explanation and being satisfied with my answer. My ideal version of happiness is not having to answer to anyone and to be my own boss (not just for work, but in general) so that I can live life the way I chose. Happiness is loving people and having them accept me for who I am and to allow myself to feel loved in return. I feel very fortunate to say that I do have all the above, am truly happy, and love the journey I am on.

Writing Exercise:

Write an essay on what your ideal version of happiness is.

____

____

____

CHAPTER 8

CONNECTING WITH OTHERS

The Importance of Having Others in Our Lives

I have emphasized how important it is to be your own best friend and to learn how to love yourself. Well there is the second part to that; it is also equally important to learn how to like (and eventually love) others as well because we don't live in this world alone. We do sometimes "need" people for certain things and that is not a contradiction to what I said prior. If you never shared your thoughts or experiences with others, of course you could still survive and take care of yourself, but how lonely that would be. We definitely need ourselves primarily, but having people in our lives gives us the sounding board and the mirror to reflect back in order to adopt a new perspective on life. Remember that in the end, we are remembered by those we left behind, and how we are remembered depends not on how we feel about ourselves (which is still important to us while we are alive), but to the rest of the world, it is how we made others feel.

<u>Writing Exercise:</u>

How do you want to be remembered by others?

____

____

____

Liking Others Makes You More Likeable

Every human being is special in their own way, but many have not been encouraged to find their uniqueness, passion, or talent. Some of us are lucky that we had parents who guided us in recognizing our strengths, which helps develop our self-esteem and drive to be ambitious. Even with that, we could all use encouragement or occasional reminders of our self-worth. We all have been guilty of either judging ourselves or others too harshly, and although we may not mean to, it happens.

Be cautious of being overly critical and using unfair comparisons that don't even make sense, *"I'm better than you"*. What does that even mean? Holding that over others only causes you to "dismiss" people that are worthy of getting to know. Not everyone makes a good first impression. Maybe there are times you don't as well, and would feel badly if someone didn't give you a second chance just because you didn't "shine" on the first encounter. Be open to others if you want them to give you the same opportunity and respect. I believe everyone has something to offer the world. There are gifts in all of us. If you adopt this belief, you will have a much easier time making friends. Be genuine and optimistically curious about everyone you meet, until you have a reason not to. You will have much more success in widening your social circle.

People feel good when they are appreciated and surrounded by those who care and make them feel special, but it goes both ways. You don't have to fall in love with everyone you meet, but you could find positive traits and "like" more people. Doing so builds positive energy, and like a magnet, will naturally pull others toward you.

I feel fortunate to have quality friends, not just acquaintances, but people I would go out of my way to do nice gestures for, spend time listening to, and be in the moment with. To be a "people person" you genuinely have to "like people" and be interested in who they actually are, which means getting to know them on a deeper level than just the surface (*like talking about the weather*). Taking time to ask questions and share a part of who you are makes you more likeable and safer to strangers. With the exception of rare occasions where personalities clash or misunderstands cannot seem to be worked out, overall, I have found it to be a win-win to be curious, kind, and open. And with traveling, this goes a tremendously long way in a foreign and unfamiliar country, as you can imagine.

<u>Writing Exercise:</u>

What is it about people that gets your attention? Can you think of certain people in your life that you are particularly curious about and want to get to know better? What is it about them that draws you in?

Being a Good Judge of Character:
Knowing Where You Fit In And Who Fits in With You

Since everything in life is a balance, even when you try to be kind, just know and accept that not everyone will become your best friend, and there will be times when certain people give you good reason to stay clear and far away. Therefore, when deciding to befriend someone, try not to jump too quickly or too deeply before you ask yourself some logical questions.

<u>Writing Exercise</u> (For this one, repeat these question for each person you feel is questionable in your life):

1. Is this person someone who will enhance my life in a positive way?

____

____

____

2. Do I feel good about myself after spending time with this person?

____

____

____

3. Do I feel listened to, validated, and respected when I am with this person?

____

____

____

4. Will this person teach me positive things that I can learn and grow from?

____

____

____

Don't be overly trusting, but also don't be overly critical or judgmental or prematurely link them to a past relationship gone bad. Be wise and balance it with giving people a chance. Treat new people in your life as a blank slate, a fresh start. The questions above should pertain to you and them and no one else.

Nobody else can tell you who is "right" for you or who you should be friends with better than you. Learn to be a good judge of character. It is a very important skill to have because the people you chose are important, and who you allow in your inner circle could change (for better or for worse) where you end up in life.

When I plan group travel trips, I do my best to match people according to common interests and personality types. As a psychologist, having studied and worked with people on a very personal level for 30 years, I believe I am a good judge of character. I understand not everybody gets along, but building a group of people that otherwise would not have met gives me great joy, as does creating bonds between people from different walks of life. When you think about it, we are more similar than different. It is amazing to me how many places there are in the world where I felt I belonged.

To Share or Not to Share

Sometimes it is hard to know how much is appropriate to disclose to a partner, a friend or a stranger. A good gage is to make sure the playing field is equal by checking the levels of vulnerability on both sides. If you share your deepest, darkest secrets with another person and know next to nothing about them, then you shared too much, too quickly. On the other hand, if you are finding that for every share you get one in return, thus evening out the playing field, you achieve equality in vulnerability levels, which is less threatening. This is how trust is built initially and then is sustained by keeping your word and fostering mutual respect over time.

Building a relationship with someone does not, and should not, feel forced or be so quick that if feels like a race to the finish line. Not everyone needs to know everything about you. You may share some now and more later, (once trust has been established) or you may choose to not to share certain things ever. It's okay to save some things just for yourself and to hold them sacred.

Appropriate sharing is all about the right balance. Don't bottle up your feelings to the point that you are suffocating, and don't shake the bottle too much where you are exploding and drowning people with your emotional intoxication. Learn how to naturally give and take in conversation like an ebb and flow, and mastering the art of riding those waves. With practice, you will instinctively know when it feels right to share or not to share.

<u>Writing Exercise:</u>

Think about someone in your personal life who you feel knows you pretty well. Do you feel you also know them just as well? Does it feel like an equal relationship? If not, would you feel more comfortable pulling back or inviting the person more directly to open up to you?

____

____

____

Repeat these questions for different people in your life.

Group travel can be therapeutic in both learning to like others and learning to share appropriately. When you are in an environment that is built to connect others with common interests, with the expectation of creating great memories, how hard could it be to like these people and find plenty of things to talk about? It is a perfect recipe for deeper, more meaningful friendships that, if fostered, can last a lifetime.

More Productive Conversations Lead to Harmony

Deeper, more meaningful, lasting friendships can only happen if both parties can survive inevitable disagreements and unintentional hurt feelings. It is likely you will face conflicts if you plan to spend any prolonged period in someone else's presence. This is not a bad thing. Once people are comfortable being honest and genuine, the real friendship starts. In addition to sharing equally, people also need to know how to resolve conflicts fairly as their "getting to know you" conversations become more substantial.

We all get into situations where conversations are not all pleasant or welcome but yet become necessary nonetheless, so I am offering some guidelines for those challenging circumstances. In order to have productive conversations instead of arguments, where one or both people just get defensive, it is advisable to ask questions in an unassuming way. I suggest when asking questions to not do it in a threatening or critical way, but rather using a curious, "need to understand you better" kind of a way. A "getting to know you" conversation is different that a "need to understand you" conversation. The former is not necessary, but rather a way to establish a connection and possible friendship. The latter is necessary if that established friendship is going to progress and more deeply foster mutual respect. People do not need to agree on everything in order to be close friends, but close friends do need to understand and accept each other's differences.

It is so important in any relationship (be it a neighbor, friend, coworker, lover, or, *for the purpose of this book,* travel partner) to allow the other person to make their own decisions and to try to respectfully understand their reasoning. Accept that when things are tense, the other person may need space from everything, including you. Learn to be okay with that. Work through your own feelings first and, when you are clear-minded and ready to have the discussion, do not blurt out the first thought that comes to mind, but think before you speak. Consider the impact of what you are about to say would have on this person you supposedly care about (*or else you would not be having the conversation at all, right?*). Allow them time to respond to you, and really listen. Accept their answer as their truth whether you agree with it or not. Don't try to control the conversation. Be curious about their feelings and patient while they explain themselves, versus rushing them or interrupting for the sake of wanting to just unload.

Try to have a mutually respectful back and forth, give and take dialogue. It may take practice but it will be worth the effort because, even if you don't get the ultimate result you were hoping for, at least you know you gave it your best effort and didn't throw your hands in the air and walk away. Most importantly, you now have a better understanding of one another. People are much more volatile and intolerant of someone else's opinion or decision when they don't take the time to understand it. Judging without understanding can lead to horrific outcomes if they continue to go unchecked. In the most mild case it may be ridicule, but in the worst case, it could be violence and sometimes even death.

<u>Writing Exercise:</u>

Think of a time when you were afraid to ask for clarification, and because you never did, it left you feeling hurt, misunderstood, belittled, or unimportant. Imagine if you had the courage to express your feelings and ask questions in order to achieve a resolution (instead of feeling abandoned and tortured by your own assumptions). In what ways do you think the outcome would have been better?

Never underestimate the importance of diverse human beings living together in unison. Humans have an amazing ability to learn and be trained on how to agree to disagree. And isn't it better to breathe the same air in harmony than to just coexist? This is something you learn in the purest form when you travel the world!

The Outcast:
Learning to Develop Social Skills in Group Settings

Getting along with and enjoying the company of others is obviously key for a successful group trip. Although many people have no trouble mingling and even pride themselves in being the "life of the party", some people are labeled, or even label themselves as "outcasts". When you are not socialized as a child in ways your peers may have been, in adulthood you may experience social "norms" as awkward. This can be considered a "handicap" if you will, however it is one that is psychological, not physical, and can be improved.

What you tell yourself about life, other people, and yourself starts with your attitude and expectations. However, our world view is heavily influenced and taught through messages we received from our formative years up to the present. We develop coping mechanisms to survive both physically and emotionally throughout our life. Some may have worked well for a period of time, but later in life, may not be as functional. We sometimes need to re-adjust and make amendments to our coping mechanisms to better fit our current circumstances. It may even require replacing new tools in our toolbox altogether.

In the case of the outcast, they may have never learned the social skills needed to connect appropriately with others, thus having to invent the wheel for the first time. Although challenging, social interaction should be encouraged. When people get in a pattern of avoiding closeness with others out of fear of rejection and potential hurt, a self-fulfilling prophecy develops with the self-talk, "nobody likes or understands me or wants to be my friend". The reality is they are the one causing the distance by cutting off others, not the other way around. Taking on challenges and risks are essential for change, and it's okay to start slowly and work up to bigger steps as you become more comfortable. As you start to see small successes in your social interactions, your fear of rejection starts to diminish.

On the flip side, if you are a confident person and you see someone who needs a little tender-loving-care, offer a hand and make a difference in their day. You never know when one small gesture can actually change a person's life. Make a difference when you can.

Writing Exercise:

Write about a time when you felt like an outcast and what feelings came up for you. Next, write about a time that you felt the desire to go out of your way to make someone else feel welcome and what that did for your soul.

____

____

____

Making New Friends Just By Being You

Making a difference in someone else's life can be as simple as being honest with who you are and sharing that honesty with others. People typically like to be around those they trust and can often sense when a person is not being genuine. Making new friends on the platform of honest communication goes a lot further and progresses faster than when a person is holding back or trying to be a people pleaser, saying only what they think others want to hear.

Those who are socially awkward may be more comfortable with ice-breakers versus intense conversation, such as light-hearted, fun get-to-know you games. Some individuals are so worried about whether they will be liked or invited a second time that they never get relaxed enough to be themselves. In these cases, when it comes to making new friends, I would suggest focusing on the activity itself, versus whether doing the activity will lead you to a deep friendship. Let that part either happen naturally or not at all. Not to sound cliché, but if it is meant to be, it will be. Try to care more about your own fulfillment in the activity and if a friendship blossoms out of that, a bond can form. You don't need to try so hard or hold high expectations, just be who you are at your best and that will naturally attract people to you. Positive energy always does!

<u>Writing Exercise:</u>

Look back on the previous assignment that asks you to describe the traits that you like or love about yourself and ask yourself if these are also things you would like in a friend. Reflect on your answer here.

Being Selective About Your Travel Partners

Deciding who to spend your precious time with is critical, and in an organized group travel trip it's just as important as where the group will be traveling to. Thus, one of the most important traits in choosing travel partners is to select friends or people you know to be reliable and are able to commit to things. There is nothing worse than planning a trip and not collecting payment in time or having people flake on you. So, number one is to invite people you trust to show up, and two, have people that know how to let go and have fun! It is also important to have people that know how to be flexible for the unexpected, which is inevitable while traveling.

There are times where it is necessary to be more direct with friends especially when it comes to making plans, even simple ones like getting together for lunch or dinner. I have noticed two categories of friends. One category includes people who are planners, who can get back to you almost immediately or within a day or two with a definitive "yes" or "no". The other category are those that just can't seem to commit or respond in a timely manner. Being a good friend, to me, means you make time for each other. Even though we are all busy in our activities and responsibilities, we can learn to maintain a balance and include those we care about. It is possible to fulfill your own needs and still leave room for others.

For the friends who disappoint you, you have a choice to either get upset or accept them for who they are and not take it personally. Some may genuinely love your friendship and thoroughly enjoy spending time with you, but just cannot organize or control enough aspects of their life or set boundaries with others to make it happen. You always have a choice of who to include or exclude in your life. Sometimes it makes sense to let go as opposed to staying angry. Holding grudges does not do any good and all it does is hurt you more than anyone else.

Moving on is liberating and focusing on people who are on the same page as you is a lot less stressful. Find a solid circle of friends to share lasting memories with. For me, this concept has and is becoming increasingly important. Vacations are supposed to be stress free and fun. Being in beautiful, stress-free places releases your soul and allows you to experience activities you would not ordinarily do. It challenges you and expands your mind and is enhanced by the people you chose to travel with. You may select travel partners ahead of time or you may meet the most amazing fellow travelers on the journey you both chose to be on. When the trip goes well, you know you were meant to be together.

I have found that the friends you make while traveling are different than the friends you meet in everyday life. When you make friendships in a foreign place, you are more open and curious and allow yourself the time and freedom to be who you really want to be, as opposed to who you have to be in your everyday life.

<u>Writing Exercise:</u>

Reflect on the last essay and how it relates to the friendships in your life? Are you currently holding any grudges about which you need to let go? Who in your life could you see traveling with as a positive and fulfilling experience?

Surviving A Long-Distance Relationship

Suppose you find yourself in a situation where you do connect with someone on the other side of the world, accept each other's differences, grow deeply attached, then find yourself heartbroken because the distance becomes too much to bear? Long distance relationships, especially romantic ones, have unique challenges, but there are techniques you can use that will increase the chances of sustaining them.

Surviving a long-distance relationship can be accomplished if 1) you learn to be okay with being alone and like your own company (*because, after all, you still are your own best friend*), and 2) you have a good local support system and accept you cannot just depend on one person to satisfy all of your needs. Work takes up a lot of people's day, but having hobbies and interests that lead to other activities outside of work is also a definite plus. I would suggest to do the things that make you happy and spend time with friends that are encouraging. If you feel you don't need your partner 24-7 to be happy, that's a good thing! When you finally reunite, your time together will be more appreciated and special.

Surviving a long-distance relationship is a true test of how deep and committed your love for each other is. It should give you more confidence and security, not less, that your love is strong and has the ability to withstand difficult times. It is a choice to look at the scenario as either sad, lonely, and miserable with constant fear of losing the person, or to think of it as an opportunity for growth where you can learn more about yourself. The former could destroy the relationship, whereas the latter will only make the relationship stronger.

Because it is so easy to stay connected with today's digital/social media technology, it does allow you to keep up with the physical and daily changes in someone's life without much effort. Long distance relationships do not work for everybody, and insecurities about losing that person to someone else who is closer and more physically available is an understandable dilemma. However, I believe in the saying "it is better to have loved than to not have loved at all." Nothing lasts forever in life and tomorrow is not guaranteed and yet, every day is a blessing, as is every minute you get to spend with someone you love.

<u>Writing Exercise:</u>

What are some things you can do to relieve the pain of longing to be with someone you can't currently be with?

____

____

____

CHAPTER 9

EXPLORING THE UNKNOWN

Fighting Feelings of Fear Through Our Dreams

As much as we all want to avoid it, some level of fear lives within all of us playing out in various ways. Sometimes it is obvious because we cannot contain it, whereas at other times we are not aware of our internal demons. More often than one would think, we process fear subconsciously through our dreams. Allowing unwanted thoughts to resurface, whether it's about our insecurities in a relationship or being physically attacked or harmed, is never pleasant. Dreams release these fears in a less threatening way allowing our subconscious mind to process and organize them which minimizes the potential for them to linger aimlessly while we are awake.

It is possible, with scary dreams or nightmares, to control the outcome if you learn and practice some techniques. Restful nights are so important for the purpose of linking your consciousness with your subconscious so they can be aligned. I often have my clients journal after awakening from an unpleasant dream so they can try to remember the details. Our memory capacity for dreams is not nearly as good as it is for our waking life. Once details are identified, you can analyze different symbolism and figure out what each stands for in your waking life. Making the subconscious conscious is a powerful tool for conquering fears. Once your brain is fully aligned, you can more confidently walk through that dark tunnel and approach the light on the other side.

<u>Writing Exercise</u>: (I suggest having a separate journal by your bed for this one.)

To get a better night's sleep, and to help prevent nightmares and insomnia, I suggest journaling just before bed to put closure on the day you just completed. Letting go of things you can no longer control helps with anxiety, which eases the mind for a more restful night. Making a To Do List for the next day can also be useful. With that preparation, you can put some of the "what's if's" to bed (*no pun intended*) and tackle the next day's agenda more readily. Essentially what you are doing is deleting past worries and replacing them with a new framework and mindset in the morning to help you succeed.

Embracing Life Versus Fearing Death

Fear of dying a premature death or death in general is significant for some, and causes them to be extra cautious with even minor life decisions. Although being careful makes perfect sense when it comes to true danger, some fear death so much that they no longer enjoy the brightness that life can offer. Do you find yourself doing the "what if" game constantly and spending more time worrying about things going wrong in the future, instead of all that is right in the present?

Our time here on Earth is short. The best way to live is make a difference every day, tell those you care about how you feel towards them, and recognize that being here should be thought of as a privilege, not an expectation. Adopting that perspective changes the way you think of death, from fear to feeling blessed that you are still here. It is unhealthy to worry about things you can't control in life. It is truly wasted energy and does not change the outcome whatsoever.

Worrying about what *might* happen to you or others just makes you, yourself, sick. If you are constantly concerned about something "bad" happening in your daily life, then you are not really living. Recognize that as long as you and your loved ones ARE here, enjoying them and the positive things in your life is the best use of your energy and time.

In terms of Covid, people need to do what they are comfortable doing, while considering any pre-existing health conditions that they or others in their circle have. We have been learning to live with it and, unless you choose to live in a bubble, you must take calculated risks which means you get to decide what is and is not worth doing. To live in fear every day is not healthy and it doesn't make the reality any different, it just makes it harder to deal with.

<u>Writing Exercise</u>

Since almost everything in life has some level of risk, make a list of the things worth risking for.

Letting Go of Control In Order to Gain More Control

We never will have 100% control over our lives. As we all know, reality is full of unknowns, surprises, and unexpected changes. However, some people don't trust anyone or anything but themselves and hold on to that false sense of control for dear life. The more you learn to trust things will be okay, even if they aren't for that moment, the more you will be able to manage your anxiety and minimize it. Life is only predictable to a point, the rest is chance and that is not just your world but the world we all live in and share. We are in the same boat in that we all survive in a world of unknowns every day.

If you allow yourself to let go and replace it with just "being" and letting things happen more naturally (without struggling to force things perfectly in a box), you will be happier and more relaxed. You will also be a more productive and "controlled" person because you will no longer be walking around in constant worry. Be comfortable with the unknown and trust the process. Things often work out in the end, and even when they don't, we still learn and grow.

There is power in being fully present because it allows you to be more equipped to handle the unknown and uncertainty of life. There is an added bonus if you master a <u>traveling mind</u>, which I define as: "internally growing while externally expanding and having the ability to be present wherever you are" – whether it is in your dreams, waking life, home, or across the world. With this perspective, no matter where you are, you will always feel at "home". Wherever your true self is, is right where you need to be.

<u>Writing Exercise:</u>

Think of a stressful situation that you have very little, if any, control over. Now imagine it getting sucked into a helium balloon and disappearing in the sky right before your eyes. You may at first feel nervous about it being so out of reach, but at the same time, a sense of relief in knowing you will no longer have to see it or deal with it as it leaves your vision. After meditating on this scenario, reflect on your feelings of letting go.

____

____

____

____

____

The "Comfort Zone" Fallacy

Some people are gung ho about the idea of going to faraway places and can't wait for the next opportunity, whereas others are extremely skeptical. I have been contemplating for some time what people actually mean when they say they want to stay in their "comfort zone". Is it really "comforting" or do people stay there because of an underlying fear of leaving their familiar, safe, predictable space? If so, it should be more properly labeled "safety zone", because there is nothing comfortable about living in fear.

What I believe most people mean when they say "comfort zone" is that they play it safe. They stay to themselves and the familiar even though they see the world changing around them. There are consequences when you choose not to participate - no risk, no change, no growth. Deciding to overcome your fear widens your "zone", enabling you to expand your horizons. Your world now becomes much bigger with fewer barriers. You suddenly feel free to explore the unknown without being afraid of all it has to teach us. I encourage everyone reading this to "live your life" in any way that keeps you growing.

SECTION IV

LIVE YOUR LIFE TRAVEL (LYLT)

CHAPTER 10

WHAT I OFFER MY GROUP TRAVELERS

Live Your Life Travel (LYLT)– The purpose is to provide a safe platform for which to explore new places both outside as well as within oneself alongside others who are open to establishing life-long friendships. LYLT is about taking hand-picked travelers to hand-picked places off the beaten path with activities for both solo and group discovery, beauty and serenity in nature, and accessibility to culture and local people.

More than having fun with existing friends, making new friends, and inspiring people to travel and make the most of their experience while traveling, I am looking to enhance that by creating experiences that are life changing. My vision is to create an ongoing stream of group travel trips with a combination of what I experienced with Bliss Camp Yoga Retreat, Back Stage Pass Travel, Ian's Castle Retreats, and TACI. In all arrangements, there is a commitment to show up, be present, and be open minded to grow in one way or another. I would like to couple self-reflection with unique excursion experiences by way of sharing knowledge, expertise, and talent with fellow members. My hope is to build growth-promoting group experiences that will leave people wanting more (not only for the fun of it, but also to gain more wisdom into the self). My travelers will have the unique opportunity to adopt a way of life whereby they connect with others as they continue to discover the layers of themselves. In my 55 years of life, I came to believe that "anything can exist if you create it with confidence and boldly lead the way."

Guadalupe Valley (Wine Country in Mexico)
My First LYLT Trip

August of 2022 was the first launch for LYLT and, even though there were a few glitches, it was a success. Besides seeing the 21 attendees having a great time, laughing and bonding with each other and exchanging phone numbers, I have had people ask when the next trip was and even referred their friends to inquire. What seems to be the benchmark for me in determining if a trip was successful is if you get repeat travelers. It gave me great joy to see everyone having a blast, but it did not go without first time lessons. I expected this to be the case and it was certainly a learning experience.

First of all, I realized that I needed to do a much better job at managing the alcohol consumption costs. I was so concerned about people enjoying themselves and not worrying about paying for their alcohol at the time of the festivities that I kept signing bar tabs all weekend, thinking to myself that it will all work out. This, I have learned, is not a good business model. I have since compared other group travel disclosures regarding what is and is not included and I now understand how to better manage this next time. When we checked into the resort, I had specified that each room needs to have a credit card attached for "incidentals", but I needed to be more clear. I had to go through the grueling process of asking people to later pitch in for the various bar tabs and, although the majority were more than accommodating, it was not something I wish to repeat. These are the trials and tribulations you need to experience with any new business and these types of mistakes can be costly.

Another glitch occurred because I was misinformed about having a reserved space inside one of the wineries we scheduled a tasting with. Once we arrived, they had us sitting outside for a delicious taco lunch that I arranged with everybody's preorder, but were told the actual wine tasting room inside was booked and could not accommodate our large group. This was a disappointment because the tasting room took place in a very cool cave, particularly inviting on the hot day that it was. However, everyone loved their tacos and we ended up agreeing on various bottles of wine to purchase and share, thus creating our own tasting to pair with lunch.

The ability to improvise is very important with group travel. Not everything will go as planned and sometimes you need to be spontaneous, flexible, and adaptable. This is one reason why it is important to vet people well for group trips because flexible situations call for flexible people. I will borrow an example from a Back Stage Pass Travel trip in Montana where our bus broke down and we were on the side of a two lane highway for about an hour and a half until help came for us. Although it could have been miserable as we were all getting hungry after a long day of sight-seeing, instead, we were really getting to know each other just slowing down and having time to kill while the musicians started breaking out their guitars and having singalongs on the side of the road. Although unplanned, it was still a positive and memorable experience and, because of the awesome people we were with, it actually was one of the highlights of the week.

I found that planning just enough structure to keep travelers entertained and involved with each other, but still giving them time to have their own space makes the perfect balance of connectedness and rest, relaxation and self-growth. Speaking of which, on this first trip, (and I plan to do something similar on future trips), I gave each traveler a LYLT travel bag which I ordered in turquoise blue with my logo on it. Each bag was filled with goodies from snacks to practical travel gadgets including a bright yellow luggage tag also with my logo. Another important item in these bags was a notebook that I labeled as an LYLT journal and inside I enclosed the following journal prompts.

I left space here for you to fill in your answers so that you could participate in this exercise in the comfort of your home, or wherever you happen to be in this moment:

1. Travel boosts brain health and also decreases a person's risk of heart attack and depression. Going to new and different places stimulates the brain.

Where are some places you would like to travel to?

____

____

____

2. Where in the world do you feel happiest? Where is your safe place?

____

____

____

3. When was the last time you experienced so much joy that you lost track of time?

____

____

____

4. What are your hobbies? Passions? Enjoyable activities?

____

____

____

5. Reflect and write about what's on your bucket list.

____

____

____

In the middle and at the end of our trip, I gave people time to share their responses with one another. This provoked people to think about how to spend their free time and it was also helpful for me in planning future trips.

The Types of Places I Prefer for Groups

When it comes to group travel, I tend to prefer less touristy places (as opposed to places that everyone goes, such as The Eiffel Tower in Paris). I have been to many popular places in the world but doing those types of activities with a large or even medium sized group seems to add unnecessary complications. I prefer to have a low stress experience for myself and my travelers so the locations I chose for group experiences versus individually or with my partner may differ.

I, of course, encourage people to see the sites of the world that are common as well as those off the beaten path because many of them have good reason to be crowded. What I often suggest is to plan those trips around (either before or after) my group travel trips if time and money allows. As you have seen, I actually do that for myself when I either attend other group travel trips or plan my own group travel trip. For instance, with the Netherlands, Germany, France, and Switzerland trip with Back Stage Pass in 2022, Jeff and I first traveled on our own all over the Netherlands, met the group in Germany, and then went on to Switzerland for a few days afterward. We did the typical tourist things in the different countries but I also used those trips as "research" for what cool places off the beaten path I could take my future LYLT people. The world has endless possibilities and I am always humbled by what I do not know every time I enter a new territory.

What Makes LYLT Unique

I am a trusted source and someone who not only has extensive travel experience and is skilled at planning unique itineraries, but also has 30 years of professionally understanding human beings and how they interact. You will not only have wonderful pictures and great food, but I will personally select individual and/or couples using my interview and "matchmaking" skills to form intimate groups of eight-twelve people who will likely become lifelong friends.

Most group travel companies are not going to take the time to pull a group of individuals that have common goals, compatible personalities, and similar travel etiquette. I work hard to create a sense of family with mutual respect and consideration of each person's individual needs to the best of my ability for the purpose of making it a positive experience for everyone. Companies that take busloads of people and extend their trips publicly to whomever signs up with their deposit first will not be able to ensure that you will get along or like the people with whom you will be traveling. I think this aspect is important to spend time on before putting a group of strangers together. I use a questionnaire to help with the screening process. Some questions I ask applicants for a LYLT trip are the following:

1. When you think of getting away, do you mostly envision a " relaxing vacation" to unwind and decompress from everyday stress or a "sightseeing trip" to experience things you don't get to do every day? If both, do you try to do a little of each on the same trip or do you concentrate on one or the other?

2. Do you like to move from place to place and cover lots of ground or have one home base and do more day excursions without covering as much distance?

3. Have you had many travel experiences in your life? Were they mostly domestic or international? Which do you prefer and why?

4. Do you tend to get along well with most people or do you prefer certain types of people over others? If so, what traits do you most like in people?

5. What do your closest friends most admire about you?

6. Do you consider yourself more of a leader or a follower?

7. Do you like to figure things out on your own or do you prefer to have others you trust help you?

8. How many "close" friends do you have? What constitutes being a "close" friend versus the relationships you have with other people in your life?

9. What do you think is the ideal number of people for a group trip?

10. Are you more a morning person or night person? What is your typical wake/sleep cycle?

11. Are you comfortable in your own company or do you feel most comfortable with others around you?

12. Do you like to experience new things or do you prefer things you already know are great?

13. Do you enjoy drinking alcoholic beverages or using any other recreational substances more than usual when on vacation or about the same as when you are home? Would you consider yourself abstinent, a light, moderate, or heavy drinker? If you are comfortable sharing, do you partake in any other recreational substances?

14. Are you in good health and enjoy being physically active or do you have limitations and prefer to do lower levels of physical activity?

15. What are your food preferences and do you have any dietary restrictions?

____

____

____

16. What would an ideal group travel trip look like to you?

____

____

____

17. What do you hope to get out of traveling with others?

____

____

____

That connection and being in the here and now is a big part of what my group travel enthusiasm is all about. It's about being able to sustain a lifestyle where I bring kind, open, interesting, and fun people together to share an experience that they otherwise would not have. I bring interactive games to loosen people up as they are getting acquainted and create an environment where people are comfortable being themselves. A place where both belly laughter and tears are welcome, and a sense of "family" encouraging belongingness and acceptance is evident.

The vetting part of my group travel preparation is important because in addition to the unique and beautiful places to which we travel, the people are what make the trip most memorable. I strive to create a cohesive and comfortable environment with a fun and interesting trip itinerary.

CHAPTER 11

SAMPLE ITINERARIES
PLACES I HAVE RESEARCHED AND/OR TRAVELED TO THAT HAVE OR CAN BE INCORPORATED INTO GROUP TRAVEL

I actually get great joy, even if it takes me many hours, out of planning trip itineraries. The added benefit of reading this book is that you have the option of taking any of these itineraries and making it your own, revising it as you see fit, or deciding to join a future LYLT! As long as I am fostering curiosity for travel in whatever form; solo, family, or group, I have accomplished what I set out to do.

The first one I will share was my very first LYLT trip (the one I spoke of in the last chapter). I purposely left the details for you to see what the actual travelers on this trip received a few days prior to our departure:

Itinerary For LYLT Summer Guadalupe Valley Trip 2022!

Friday, August 5th 2022

9:45am –Van pick up.
Drive to **Guadalupe Valley** via the Tecate Border (please bring Passports).

1:00pmish – Arrive at <u>Ojo Azul Resort</u> – check into rooms and relax by the pool!

2:30pm – 4:30pm Massage appointments for whomever booked in advance.

4:30-5:15pm – Rachel's free stretch class for anyone who wants to participate.

6:30pm – Happy Hour in the Sky Bar with complimentary welcome drinks of your choice!

8:00pm – Family Style Dinner in the Vineyards followed by:

Fun and games by the Firepit

The Resort's Live Entertainment

<u>Saturday, August 6th 2022</u>

Have your Complimentary Breakfast Buffet.

10:30am – Wine Tour Van Pick Up to 3 wineries including lunch.

6:00pm – Return to Ojo Azul Resort.

6:45pm – Van leaves for those with dinner reservations at <u>Deckman's and Bajaonskase</u> *(Both outstanding atmosphere and high end delicious steak and seafood or Japanese cuisine, respectively).*

9:30pm- Approximate arrival back to Ojo Azul.

<u>Sunday, August 7th 2022</u>

Complimentary Breakfast Buffet between 8:00am and Noon.

8:30am – 9:15am Rachel's free exercise class.

9:30am – 11:30am massages for those with appointments.

11:30am – Special Cava Wine Tasting at Ojo Azul.

1:00pm – Van leaves for Tecate.

2:00pm – Goodbye Group Lunch at <u>El Lugar De Nos in Tecate</u> (*which was a very cool atmosphere with interesting eclectic décor*).

3:30pm – Van leaves to cross the border to return to San Diego.

5:30pm/6:00pm – Estimated arrival to San Diego.

4-Day Cancun Trip for Couples

Below is a trip I planned (without the host service) for a first-time-traveling-together couple in 2021. I booked all flights, accommodations, and excursions and provided recommendations for leisure activities and restaurants in the area. This itinerary, now that it has been tested and successful, now is a suggested itinerary for future planning. Here is what I provided this couple:

Day 1 - Check into Beach Palace Resort All Inclusive.
Blvd Kukulcan Km 11.5, Hotelera Zone, Cancun, QROO

Suggested Restaurant for dinner: Tequila International Cuisine Buffet (at your hotel).

If you want a spa treatment or massage at your hotel, I recommend you book it in advance.

Nearby points of interest:
La Isla Shopping Mall – 8 min walk
Cancun Interactive Aquarium – 8 min walk
Marlin Beach – 10 min walk

Day 2 –
7:30am – Get free breakfast (included at hotel).
8:30am Be at pick up spot.

9:00am – 11:00am – Cancun Jungle Tour Adventure with Speedboat and Snorkeling. Suggestions for lunch: La Bamba or Kosher Hotspot
Dinner: Fantino or Unami

Day 3 -
Get free breakfast at your hotel early and get picked up from hotel lobby.
8:00am – 8:00pm Chichen Itza, Cenote & Valladolid All-Inclusive Tour with buffet lunch included.

If you are hungry for dinner when you return, besides your hotel's 4 restaurants, you can also order delivery from Kosher Hotspot if you haven't tried it yet.

<u>Day 4</u> -
Get free breakfast at hotel and be ready outside hotel lobby at 12:10pm
1:30pm – 5:30pm <u>ATV, Ziplining & Cenote Tour w/ snorkeling at Extreme Adventure Eco Park</u>.

Suggested Restaurants for dinner: Either Fantino or Unami

<u>Description of Recommended Restaurants:</u>

<u>Tequila Buffet</u> – in your hotel, international cuisine and casual. Nice for your first night to settle into your resort.

<u>La Bamba</u> – Mex-Seafood (good seafood with local flavors).
5m 51 Blvd Kukolkan Km 9.5 Local 11-C 77500
Recommend for Friday lunch or Friday or Sunday dinner
Reservations recommended.

<u>Fantino</u> – High end/Fancy European Restaurant (in the Ritz Carlton with nice decor and excellent food).
Rtno, del Rey 36, Zona Hotelera
Recommended for Friday or Sunday dinner (Check on live entertainment for each night).
Reservations necessary.

<u>Kosher Hotspot</u> – Israeli Kosher food, large portions/reasonable prices/high ratings.
Kosher Blvd, Kukulcan 9 in Plaza Caracol
Recommended for Friday lunch or Saturday late night delivery to your hotel (check hours).

<u>Unami</u> – Japanese Teppanaki where they cook in front of you/great reviews.

In the Hotel NYX, Blvd Kukulkan 11.5 Interior, Zona Hotelera
Recommended for Friday or Sunday dinner unless you want more local faire.
Reservations recommended.

Other Future Group Travel Itineraries

I went through and revised itineraries I have either used before for Jeff and me, or planned for a future trip not yet taken with group travel in mind. The plan along with my commentary should give you an idea of what a group travel trip would look like for any number of locations.

22-Day Europe Trip of 2018
Tour of Greece, Sicily, Southern Italy, Croatia, & France

Day 1 -We left on a Wednesday, flew out of San Diego to San Francisco International Airport and then took a direct flight to Istanbul (fourteen hours) and then a shorter flight to Athens, Greece and stayed one night at a place called *Cozy Apartment near the airport* (on Booking.com) for one night. Tel: + 30 694 875 1840 / 5 Galileou, Artemis 190 16, Greece - for $73 a night at the time. (*This place was really cute and in walking distance to a local restaurant / bar but definitely on the outskirts of the city in a quiet suburb just to sleep before a 45 min flight to the island of Santorini at 5:15am the next morning. Aegan Airlines is one of the local airlines and we flew then for $61 per person.*)

Day 2 - **Santorini** was a beautiful and amazing place to visit, just like the pictures with all white buildings against a deep blue sea. We walked the Caldera to Fira (sights on the way/ tourist port town with donkeys). (*If I were to go back, I would stay in an area called Imerovigli along the Caldera– an upscale, central town with restaurants all lined up*).

<u>Day 3</u> – We explored the beaches and found an area where you can purchase a lounge chair with food and beverage (which would be affiliated with whatever hotel/restaurant was across the street from that particular section of the beach). It was a wonderful way to spend part of our day.

After a half day of exploring the beach areas, we checked out <u>Boutari Winery</u> and <u>Santorini Brewing Company</u>. Boutari Winery had a nice wine tasting that we enjoyed. (*We didn't end up going sailing and snorkeling as planned this trip, but would highly recommend doing so on this beautiful island and would definitely plan an excursion for a group to do this activity in the future*).

We had a wonderful dinner in <u>Oia</u> on the point and watched the unmatched beautiful sunsets. (*It is a quieter side of the island than Fira (which is more touristy and lively) but there are many nice accommodations in Oia and some prefer that vibe*).

<u>Day 4</u>- We flew into Athens and then to **Palermo** (the largest city in Sicily), looked around and then drove to **Erice** (*a very memorable and unique place which lay on top of a steep hilltop town with medieval streets about one hour and fifteen minutes from Palermo*). We stayed right in the heart of the village in a Condo/Hotel which I would highly recommend called <u>Erice Pietre Antiche</u> – (Via Giuseppe Fontana,12, Erice, 91016 Italy) Tel: 39 (347) 2633599 for only $147.86 a night at the time.

<u>Day 5</u> - We explored the coastal route (four hours to <u>Cerafu beach</u> town for lunch) on the way to **Taormina** (mountain-top town overlooking Sicily's most famous resort).

There we stayed at the <u>Hotel Ariston & Palazzo Santa Caterina</u> (Via Bagmoli Croce, Taormina, ME, 98039) for two nights at $161 a night. Tel: 39 (0942) 6190. (*It was in a good location in walking distance, although very hilly there, to restaurants and shopping*). We enjoyed about a day and a half there, eating delicious food, walking the hilly neighborhoods, and took the cable down to the bottom where the beaches are.

On this particular day, I remember it was pouring rain and we helped an old Italian woman sweep the water out of her store (partly to help her out and partly as an excuse to keep dry). She was very gracious and started to open up to me about her troubles once she learned I was a psychologist. Even though we barely understood each other due to the language barrier, there was a special emotional connection.

Day 6 - After our stay in Taormina, we drove to Catania in the late afternoon to explore and shop (cheaper than Taormina) and had dinner before dropping off the car. We then took an overnight train to Naples (*which was interesting because at some point in the night the train actually goes on a track onto a ferry and then back on land again*). Once in Naples (where you must try the Neapolitan pizza) we took a local train to **Sorrento** (one of my favorite places in Italy). The next time going there, I would recommend looking into Air BNB's in a nice neighborhood within walking distance to everything, or for a group trip, I would find a boutique hotel near the old town area.

Day 7 – We did the most amazing excursion experience that I would, hands down, take any group tour. It was called the Gastronomic Farm Tour (see the information below for future reference). It was described as a five and a half hour farm experience with tastings, pizza making, and limoncello, but it was actually so much more than that. We got picked up in a little tuk-tuk motorized vehicle and rode it down these windy, narrow streets which was a thrill in itself. We were greeted with a huge charcuterie board of delicious snacks and a glass of fresh limoncello. We saw animals, watched them make fresh mozzarella cheese, and toured the different areas of the farm which was quite interesting and educational. When it came to making the pizza, it was definitely the highlight as we literally tossed and caught our pizza dough in mid-air! They even videotaped it in slow motion for us to have as a keepsake.

Gastronomic Farm Tour (5.5 hour/farm experience) Viator –
6517FOOD)
Contact-Gialpi DMC on IT+39 081872 4372

<u>Day 8</u> - The next morning we took a ferry to **Capri** (about 20-50 minutes depending on which ferry you select). It is very beautiful, a little more upscale than Sorrento but worth a day or two. We stayed at one of many nice places (<u>Villa San Felice</u>, Via Li Campi 13, Capri, NA 80073 Tel: 39 (081) 8376122 $251.54 for one night at the time).

Our plan was to explore Capri, the Blue Grotto, and maybe Anacapri. We ended up not doing the Blue Grotto because we had limited time and since that was one of the main tourist attractions, the lines were very long. However, we did take a single seated chairlift up to the very top of Anacapri and it was very memorable and not something all tourists do, but I would definitely repeat it again and take a group there (in addition to seeing the Blue Grotto) next time. Capri is a must see and it was there that I had the best risotto I ever tasted.

<u>Day 9</u> - We left our hotel around 7:45am to get ferry to Naples then to the airport for an hour long flight to **Dubrovnik, Croatia**. I highly recommend where we stayed at the <u>Secret Apartments</u> for three nights, Zeljarica 3, Dubrovnik, 20000 Croatia for $625.89 at the time. (*However with a group I would need to find accommodations with more rooms, although I still like the idea of being within the old city walls in a historic building as the one we stayed in.*)

Things to do right in the heart of Dubrovnik are: the <u>City Walls</u>, where you can walk the circumference above the large medieval village and make stops for drinks at the bars along the way if you choose; the <u>Old Town</u> below the city walls where there is a plethora of restaurants, shops, and entertainment day and night. The Game of Thrones is what made this place famous so you will see plenty of evidence of that, but you need not be a fan to find it a fascinating place and probably one of the best kept medieval cities in the world. I suggest visiting sooner rather than later as with the growing recognition, it will only become more crowded. (*This is one of the very special places I look forward to traveling to with groups and actually have one planned for June of 2024*).

<u>Day 10</u> - I highly recommend taking a fifteen min ferry from Old Town to the island of **Lokrum** (where peacocks and rabbits run wild and it's the biggest park in the area). I was amazed by the beauty and the variety of what you actually can see and do on that small island. You can hike, swim, eat and drink, and see nature all in a few hours. I also recommend our other activity of the day which was taking the cable car up to **Mt. Srd** to see gorgeous views of the luxury hotels, the medieval walled city, and Adriatic sea. Other, more simple areas to explore are – Old Port for people watching, ice cream at Dolce Vita, and a sunset drink at the Dubrovnik Cliff bar.

<u>Day 11</u> - We spent a whole day and evening exploring a nearby island called **Korkula.** It is a two and a half hour ferry ride each way from Dubrovnik and I call it a mini Dubrovnik with cobblestone streets and wineries where we spent a lovely day walking around and had a romantic dinner. (***Miljet*** *is another small island that is only one hour each way on the ferry. It boasts of a beautiful, green National Park which we did not make it to on our first trip to Croatia, but there are numerous islands to see so each time you can add different ones which makes it a place you would want to go back to*).

<u>Day 12</u> - The next day we picked up a rental car (and driving in Croatia is so easy and smooth). We drove to one of my favorite towns – **Zadar,** with a short stop in **Split** along the way (the whole distance from Dubrovnik is five and a half hours). Split is a major city, more modern that Dubrovnik but also has an Old Town section and an international airport as well.

<u>Day 13</u> - The sites to see in Zadar (besides their Old Town restaurant/shopping area right near the water) are the <u>Sea Organ</u> – architectural art object that plays sounds by sea waves under marble steps, and <u>The Greeting or Monument to the Sun</u>. (*These areas bring*

the whole community together, both tourists and locals, and I loved the vibe and friendly atmosphere so it is a definite for my next Croatia group travel trip. I plan to book a boutique hotel right in the heart and in walking distance to the areas mentioned above).

<u>Day 14</u> - From Zadar, the next morning we drove to **Plitvice Lakes National Park** (one and a half hours). We checked into the <u>Rustic Lodge Plitvice</u>, Plitvice Jezera /Jezera, Plitvice jezera licko-senjska 53231 ($129.82 at the time). (*I do recommend this accommodation for a quaint, family owned Air BNB type stay). It was here that we played Yambi (the Croatian version of Yahtzee) for the first time.*

Plitvice was breathtaking. Seeing pictures of the turquoise water and greenery with robust waterfalls was one of the driving forces that made me travel all the way to Croatia and I was the opposite of disappointed! It was beyond beautiful. The hiking was fairly easy (with optional challenges) with wildlife, bridges, and even ferries from one location to another. If that wasn't enough, it even had a few restaurants and bars. It really has something for everyone there.

<u>Day 15</u> - We left Croatia from the Zagreb airport (a two hour drive from Plitvice) to **Nice, France** with a three hour and 45 min layover in Barcelona (*not enough time to go explore but we did experience that beautiful city on a different trip*).

We stayed in a great apartment for two nights that I found called <u>Massena Square</u> (4 Place Messena, Nice Provence-Alpes-Cote-DAzur 06300 for $235.43 at the time. Property manager tel: +33—628502550

What I liked about the place was that it was perfectly situated in the heart of <u>Old Town</u>, and it was spacious for two people. (*Please note that it had four flights of stairs and no elevator, as many buildings in Europe do not have.*) For a group I would find a boutique hotel with more rooms but still very close to that area.

Day 16- We ventured on top of the mountaintop to a town called **Eze** the next day for lunch and to explore the cobblestone streets and the Parfum Museum, where I still to this day will order a favorite perfume I fell in love with called Cantebell. From there we took the train to **Monte Carlo, Monaco** to see where the famous car racing takes place (the tracks were clearly marked!). We had an amazing Indian dinner in one of the restaurants along the track. Of course the casino there is a big draw and it's like a museum inside and worth going into even if you don't want to risk your luck.

Day 17 - The next day we strolled around Nice until it was time to catch our flight to our next destination. This portion of our trip was the French castle retreat as explained it in Chapter 6. **Romenay** is the closest town to it, and it is a lovely, quaint, non-tourist town such that many people do not speak anything other than French, yet are very friendly. They have a wonderful farmers market on certain days with not just food, clothing, and arts and crafts, but to my surprise they also had livestock for sale (chickens, ponies, and other animals). The name of the castle is Chateau de Montsymond, in an even smaller town called Vescours. If you google it, you will be amazed that we got to call it "home" for so many years.

Day 21 - After four wonderful days at the castle, we took a train from Lyon to **Paris** (about a three hour ride) and stayed in a hotel in the Latin district (*which is my personal favorite area of Paris*) at the - Relais Hotel Du Vieux Paris, 9 Rue Git Le Coeur, Paris, Tel: 33 144321590. (*I leave this information for you because it was a pleasant experience and the staff there were very friendly, but I chose not to necessarily bold it since there are so many options to choose from that I would probably want to switch it up next time. It was there that I spent my actual 50th birthday however!*)

We spent the evening with some castle friends who were also in Paris with us and enjoyed a river cruise (which I highly recommend) and ended it in a cool jazz club situated in a cave.

<u>Day 22</u> - The next day our three week plus vacation ended as we flew out of Charles de Gaulle airport to fly back to San Diego via Frankfurt on one of my favorite airlines Lufthansa (overall flight time is thirteen hours and 25 minutes). As I mentioned before, that is my relaxation time of reading, movies, and writing, so the time flies as I fly, (*no pun intended*).

18-Day Europe Trip of October 2021
Tour of Ireland, Vienna, & Prague

This trip was very fun and it was my first time in Ireland (another favorite country now). It was a great time of year to go weather-wise (with the exception of Galway as it is more north and rainy) and a little less crowded with tourists which is why we usually choose this time of year for travel in Europe.

<u>Day 1</u> -We took a red eye flight through Chicago and arrived at 9:00am in Dublin then drove two and a half hours to **Galway**. We enjoyed walking along the waterfront and into the <u>Latin Quarter </u>in the old town area. It was very lively with restaurants, bars, and nightlife.

<u>Day 2</u> - After a half day more in Galway, we headed out to **Dingle** (a three hour drive with a rest stop in city of Limerick, one hour on the way). Dingle had cobblestone streets with colorful restaurants and pubs (some lively spots were Benny's Pub, O'Sullivan's Courthouse, The Dingle Pub).

<u>Day 3</u> – Drove through **Slea Head Drive** which is a must see and Ireland's most scenic drive with small Irish-speaking villages and Hollywood scene spots to take in, so as you can imagine, there were many beautiful picturesque stops. (*We did it as a great half day excursion but next time around with a group I would like to take in one of the nice restaurants for lunch or dinner that we didn't know existed on our first visit. A nice boutique hotel away from the crowds for the night would be my preference the second time around*).

<u>Day 4</u> - The next day we drove one hour to **Killarney National Park** and stayed in Killarney, one of my favorite inland towns in Ireland, and spent the day there. (*What I would love to do next time is take a group and spend a few days driving around the entire* <u>*Ring of Kerry*</u> *to see more of the national park and waterfalls. I would book our overnight stay on the other side by* <u>*Waterville*</u>*, a quaint town and the only one that sits right on the water, and enjoy swimming and other water activities in one of the warm summer months. Apparently Charlie Chaplin used to go here with his family and there now is a statue of him as well as a comedy festival in his honor every August.*)

<u>Day 5</u> - Drove to **Clonakilty** (two hours and fifteen min drive) and stayed in a rather interesting accommodation called <u>Un Ullord-Pod Camping Clonakilty </u> which was a tiny home on a small farm with animals. (*They had maybe four or five of them so for a small group it could be fun to buy out the place*). Another hotel in that area that would be a good option is <u>Fernhill House and Gardens</u> where we just stopped by for a drink but it was a very classy sitting on top of a hill with gorgeous views of landscaping below.

<u>Day 6</u> - I am really into miniature things so we went to the <u>West Cork Model Railway Village</u> which had a model running train around the little villages that were in the Cork area of Ireland and many of them were places that we had visited or drove through so it was interesting to see them again in miniature form. (*I would not highly recommend it if it was not on your route already and I would rather take a group elsewhere to be honest, but I enjoyed it and it was a good time killer before we could check into our next Airbnb*).

We only had a short drive 45 minute drive that day to **Kinsale**, a nice small town/fishing village right on the water with a harbor full of boats and wonderful restaurants. It was a romantic and fairly quiet town but offered enough to enjoy a night out and walk around the many shops. That night we stayed at an Airbnb on another farm, but this one did not have animals. What it did have was a wonderful Irish lady who treated us like family in her two story home.

<u>Day 7</u> – We started our day with a <u>Jameson Whiskey Tour</u> in the Cork region which was a good tour and then headed into **Dublin** and checked into the <u>Zanzibar Locke Apartments</u>, just steps from the <u>Ha' Penny Bridge</u> connecting to <u>Temple Bar area</u>. It was a nice, clean, modern hotel in a great location that I would book for a group.

<u>Day 8</u> - For first timers, I would definitely recommend the Hop On and Off Bus to explore different sights of the city as we did. We went to many places, one included a <u>Guinness Beer Brewery Tour</u>.

Hop On and Off Buses are very common in bigger cities all over the world and generally they make sense as it gives you a great lay of the land and flexibility of spontaneously hopping off at any given stop to see something you want to explore up close. Situations where I would not recommend them in is if the traffic on the streets is heavy and there is easy and accessible underground transportation instead. We often found our way around big cities in Europe by taking the subway or metro system and it gave us a more local feel as well. Public transportation also gives you more flexibility to not have to go on the bus's time schedule, and although buses are usually pretty frequent, subways, trains, and metros are usually much more efficient.

<u>Day 9</u> - It is always nice to get away from the city and make your way to one of the islands (**Dalkey/Howth/Malaheid**). We enjoyed Dalkey, where many wealthy celebrities have homes, and we saw some amazingly beautiful ones. Matt Damon and his family lived there for a while and we saw a glimpse of their estate, but it was mostly covered by trees. We found Howth particularly worthy of an overnight trip (*next time around since we didn't know how nice it was*) and it is easy and quick to get there by train. (It was there that I had got over my resistance to eating a whole fish (eyes and all), often it's a Branzino, but this time it was a Dover Sole, and it was delicious).

<u>Day 10</u> - We flew to **Vienna, Austria**, which is definitely a livable place in my eyes. We stayed at a fabulous Apartment in the <u>Nebau neighborhood</u> which was great and the apartment was well

decorated. It was nice staying in a neighborhood where locals live versus other areas where there are big, corporate hotels and swarms of tourists. (*For a group, I would look for a boutique hotel in this or a similar neighborhood with easy access to desirable sites. The public transportation is very easy to use in this wonderful city*).

Day 11 - One of the highlights for me as a psychologist was the visit to the Sigmund Freud Museum, where I spent a good three or four hours and learned a great deal about this interesting and brilliant contributor to the field of psychology, whom is often referred to as "The Father of Psychology". Afterwards, we visited the nearby parks Volksgarten and Burggarten (Palm House, Butterfly House, Coffee House/Restaurant), and checked out the old town area that evening.

Day 12- We walked around Museum Quarter and ate in one of the Hidden Gardens (which are restaurants behind some of museums or buildings that you may not see right off the main street). We took an Uber to Prater Park which was an amazing amusement park with a variety of adult and kid rides set in a beautiful setting with really good restaurants as well. (*I would definitely take a group there for a half a day*).

Afterwards, we took a long walk along the Danube River and saw the Floating Gardens. It was a very fun area where there were restaurants on either side of the river and locals enjoyed hanging out and teenagers rode skateboards in the skatepark along the water. It was an overall nice vibe, and a pleasant way to end the day.

Day 13 - On this day, we got picked up at 9:00am sharp by a driver for a sightseeing/daytrip to Prague with stops scheduled at Mikulov and Kunta Hora.

Before I go into detail about this awesome day, I want to mention that I cannot recommend the DayTrip Service enough. It is a service where you select your pick up/ drop off destination as well as any of the stops on the route listed as options for an additional fee. The driver also acts as a tour guide for each destination. We had a wonderful driver named Mike who spoke perfect English and lived in a town outside of Vienna, but spent a lot of his formative years living with family in Los Angeles. We got to know him pretty well over the five or six hours in the car as well as the sightseeing and wine-tasting we did with him. He actually loved my music as I shared a few songs with him on the long car drive and he kept wanting me to play "just one more" until we exhausted my whole album. I was touched by that and it made that car ride very memorable for me. We have kept in touch since that visit.

Mikulov was an old Jewish village where a lot of history took place and Mike did a great job educating us. We were supposed to make a stop at Kunta Hora as well, but were so consumed with the first stop that we did not want to rush our time there. This is what flexibility while traveling is all about and I have no regrets.

We arrived in **Prague** at the <u>House At The Big Foot B&B</u> which I highly recommend for the staff hospitality, the custom-made breakfast, and the location. Prague is a beautiful place with beautiful people, inside and out. They are warm and good spirited.

Prague is one of the only cities that survived the Holocaust for a bittersweet reason. Hitler, himself, admired the city as a place in which he had personal interest in living, and therefore, his orders were to preserve it for selfish reasons. Nevertheless, it is a desirable city and we were blessed to have the opportunity to see it as it once was. It has an amazing trolley system and we learned our way around the whole city, sometimes getting lost, but we enjoyed the adventure.

<u>Day 14</u> - That Sunday we enjoyed our lovely B&B breakfast with eggs cooked to order, and we met this really lovely couple who were visiting from The Netherlands. (*As a side note, we got to know them well enough to stay in touch, and a year later, visited them in their home in the Netherlands. Soon, they will be flying out to the states partially to attend our wedding! Again reiterating another example of life-changing and growing friendships that develop because of traveling.)*

Later that morning we went on a two hour guided tour of the city on Harley Treks. We had lunch at the historic <u>Strahov Monastic Brewery</u>, where I had a remarkable lunch of onion soup made with beer, steak and chips. We saw the gardens below <u>Prague Castle</u> and checked out the <u>Farmer's Market</u>.

<u>Day 15</u> – Using the trolley system, we explored <u>Nove Mesto (New Town)</u> and visited the Czech Repubrick (Lego museum), Gallery of Steel Figures, and Museum of the Senses. We then freshened up and walked around Stare Mesto (Old Town) in the evening for dinner and nightlife. <u>Josefov</u> – the Jewish community, is in the heart of old town and there were many great restaurants to choose from.

<u>Day 16</u> - Our plan was to go to <u>Terezin Concentration Camp</u>, but we had a glitch. We ended up getting a late start because we were trying to ship a few bottles of wine, which I would not have bothered with if I knew then what I know now.

Here is the story and lesson learned. It posed to be a very expensive ordeal and difficult to find the nearest post office - which ended up being within the Prague Castle of all places. After we wasted Uber fees all over town, we discovered it was not worth the money it would cost to ship the bottles because it was hundreds of dollars which greatly exceeded the value of the wine itself. We ended up giving away a bottle and snugly packing the others in our suitcases. By that time, it was getting too late to take the train to Terezin and we were told that if we didn't get back on the 4:30pm train, we would be stranded there because they do not run that late.

As a rule, it's best not to take very much alcohol home with you while traveling, even though it is tempting at times when you find gems that you cannot buy elsewhere. You have to consider the weight of your checked in suitcase because there are limits and it can get costly if you exceed that weight limit. It may not be worth the value of what you are trying to bring back. Many times you can figure out a way to have purchases shipped direct, but always decide if it is worth the cost in the end. You may also want to check to see if you can, in fact, buy it where you live.

We did recoup our day after all by going to the wonderful <u>Prague Zoo</u> which was beautiful and the animals were well taken care of. We actually really enjoyed the rest of the day, after the frustration we had to deal with. I do wish we had been able to visit Terezin but this is another example of where flexibility comes into play.

<u>Day 17</u> - We spent the morning taking our Covid test in order to fly back to the states and finished up the day revisiting our favorite sites and last minute shopping.

<u>Day 18</u> – Left @ 8:00am to fly home on 10:20am flight via Frankfurt and Seattle and arrived in San Diego at 10:34pm (it's always nice to gain a day flying home!)

20-Day Europe Trip of October 2022
Tour of The Netherlands, Luxembourg, Germany,
France & Switzerland

(*This trip was partially a couples trip and partially a group trip with Back Stage Pass Travel so I included the whole itinerary so you can see how we combined so many different types of experiences in one trip*).

<u>Day 1</u> – Left on a Friday afternoon flight to Amsterdam via Salt Lake City and arriving at 2:25pm in Amsterdam on Saturday (with about 11 hours total flying time with the latter international flight being about nine and a half hours).

<u>Day 2</u> - Checked into our Houseboat AirBNB, settled in and checked out the local neighborhood. (*This houseboat in Amsterdam stay was a bucket list item for me and if I have a do over I would choose a more populated area than Westerdok and closer to the heart of Amsterdam and in a more modern, classier houseboat*). Our host was great though and served fresh juice, pastries, and sausages every morning at 8:30am sharp.

<u>Day 3</u> – Explored **Amsterdam** w/ public transportation (*it was easy and efficient*)

<u>Dam Square</u>, ferry to <u>Nsdm Werf (Pllek bar)</u>

5:00-6:30pm – <u>Captain Jack's Canal Cruise</u> (with drinks and snacks). (*This may sound cheesy, but it was actually really fun and perfect to bring a group on as it was only an hour and a half – perfect for a Happy Hour before dinner cruise, and we could book the entire boat to ourselves.*)

<u>Day 4</u> – Explored Amsterdam on bikes (*it's a thing you do there, but actually we opted out of this idea because when we first arrived at our houseboat we witnessed a bike accident with a car involved and a girl laying on the side of the road so... we figured the trolley may be the better option for us*).

Went to <u>Heineken Brewery tour</u> (which is pretty interesting and has a lot of unanticipated special effects that are stimulating to the senses). Gustav Klint exhibit (projection of his art – in the Fabrik Lumineers area of Amsterdam). *This was a really cool exhibit where each room was in constant motion with his colorful art scenes one after another (similar to the traveling Van Gough exhibit).*

<u>Day 5</u> - Picked up rental car @ 8:30am and drove to **Zaanse Schans** – an 18th century village with windmills, cheese factory, clogs, jewelry and many other workshops and stores to buy unique gifts. (*It also had a few restaurants and a hotel on the premises. I inquired about doing a group retreat here and having them arrange a unique educational program for Live Your Life Travel.*)

Drove to **The Hague** (one hour and seven minutes from Amsterdam).

Visited <u>Maduradam</u> - miniature theme park. (*This was by far the best miniature park I have ever been to, and I have been to several because I seek them out both in the states and overseas.*) I do highly recommend it for its history and combination of old and new as well as the artistry of thousands of intricate mini buildings, vehicles, *landscaping, lakes and bridges. It all looks so real. They even have a simulator airplane ride which is really fun. I definitely think it warrants being on the group travel agenda.*

Lunch in <u>Scheveningen</u> – seaside town with a huge Ferris wheel right on the beach.

Drove to **Delft** (about 20 minutes) and checked into <u>Hotel de Koophandel</u>, (*which I highly recommend for individuals or a group because it is a quaint hotel right in the square surrounded by a great variety of restaurants just feet away. The locals also live in the apartments within that square and hang out and gather so, although you are in a hotel, you feel like a local*). The address is: Beestenmarkt 30, 2611 GC. Outside of the square we also explored the neighborhood which was very walkable (not hilly at all like so many other places in Europe).

<u>Day 6</u> - Visited the <u>Delft Pottery Factory</u> (*which was a must see if you go to Delft, as this is what gives the town it's recognition. I had no idea of the breadth of contributions that Delft was responsible for like pillars and flooring in addition to the beautiful pottery of all types. I got very excited to learn that they offer high tea time with all the fancy snacks; it would be a very special and memorable group outing.*)

Drove to **Rotterdam** (47 minutes). Checked into <u>Hotel New York</u> (*which I recommend for groups because it is historic and interesting inside, has a few fabulous restaurants, both casual and formal, and is right where the water taxis can pick you up to explore different areas of Rotterdam*). That address is: Koninginnenhoofd 1, Rotterdam, 3072 AD.

<u>Day 7</u> – Walked around the <u>Japanese Tea Garden</u> and went up to the top of the <u>Euromast</u> (*The largest tower of the Netherlands. They actually have a very nice restaurant and just a few hotel rooms you can rent and stay overnight on one the top floors! As you can imagine, the view from up there is amazing and it would be awesome to plan a group trip that involves a sunset dinner there.*)

<u>Day 8</u>- Drove to Mook (one hour and 45 minutes) (*This may not be a place I would take a group as our main purpose in going to Mook was to visit our new friends whom we met in Prague at the B&B we stayed in a year prior*). That night we stayed at the Hotel Oranjestaete in **Nijmegen** (*which is actually a very nice, spacious apartment in walking distance to the lovely college town*).

Nijmegen has some wonderful history and a combination of old and new buildings. Our friend, who grew up there, showed us an old post office literally next door to the modern portion of the post office building and explained that due to World War II, some buildings survived and others had to be rebuilt within the same block. Because Nijmegen is not in route to other places I would most likely take a group and time is always a factor, I would recommend visiting Nijmegen, if you are intrigued, as a side trip rather than with a larger group.

<u>Day 9</u> – Drove to **Luxembourg** (three hours and 22 minutes) and checked into our Airbnb apartment and explored the neighborhood (*which was in walking distance to both the upper-modern and lower-historic parts of town so we had our choice*).

<u>Day 10</u> - Explored Luxembourg on their free public transportation visited different districts such as Ville Haute, Gare, and Grund.

Luxembourg is very small but large in beauty everywhere you look. It's very green and clean with great transportation that is free to everyone. It has castles and parks along modern shopping malls and great choices for the taste buds. I would recommend it more for individual or couples traveling rather than as a group.

<u>Day 11</u> - 7:30am – Four hour drive to Basel, Switzerland with a stop in <u>Petite, France</u> for lunch in the <u>Strasbourg region</u> (*This is what I love about Europe, being able to be in 3 countries in one day with ease*). It was here at the Euro Airport Basel / Mulhouse Freiburg that we dropped off our rental car and met up with the Back Stage Pass

Travel Group for the week long Germany tour in <u>Eichstetten, Germany</u>. (*By the way, this airport I mentioned is the only one of its kind that is owned by two countries as it sits on the border of Switzerland and France. Therefore, if you have one leg in each side, you are literally standing in two countries simultaneously which, of course, the child within me had fun for a few minutes hopping back and forth.*)

<u>Day 12</u> - Enjoyed <u>Rinklin Family Winery</u> where we headquartered and hung out with Geoff Tate and the band. (*The highlight of the day was the wagon ride where the 30 of us were divided into two groups competing for who can sing the loudest while sampling various wines grown there, which was mentioned in Section Two*).

<u>Day 13</u> – **Freiburg, Germany** (medieval town) – (*Wonderful for shopping, exploring, and eating until your heart's content*).

<u>Day 14</u> – **La Montagne de Singes, France** (*An amazing sanctuary where monkeys run wild and uncaged and you can enter their world as long as you keep 6 feet away from them*).

Dinner in **Colmar, France** (*A beautiful town that borders Germany*).

<u>Day 15</u> – **Eifelpark Alpine Slides, Germany** (*We all had a blast racing each other on the various types of slides and water rides as well as virtual reality options while riding on the indoor coaster ride. They also had hiking trails and a number of different animals. It was a great place to bring a group of adults that love being kids for a day.*)

<u>Day 16</u> – **Riquwher, France** (*A gorgeous picture perfect storybook village to explore and eat wonderful food. We took a canal boat tour.*)

<u>Day 17</u>- Enjoy Eichestetten (Geoff Tate show in the evening), kind of a free day, which was nice after all the running around.

<u>Day 18</u> – Check into Airbnb apartment in **Basel, Switzerland**

Settled in and explored the neighborhood which was right along the canal and it was beautiful. Nearby there was a popular coffee shop where locals hung out and played board games. There were even a few musicians that broke out their guitars and sang. I love when I pick the perfect "home feel" type of neighborhood.

Day 19 – Sightseeing in Basel, Switzerland (explored old town). Basel is a beautiful city and we did so much walking, eating, and shopping 'til our hearts were content. I did not know that prostitution was legal there. They actually had a block where the sidewalks were marked with circles with a female body figure inside indicating that this is where the women needed to stand when they were soliciting business.

Day 20 – 10:15am Flight home via Amsterdam and Atlanta. Arrived home in San Diego around 9:35pm.

18-Day Trip for New Zealand and Australia- (Was planned for Winter of 2019)

This next trip itinerary is one that I had planned but never came to fruition because the pandemic occurred when we would have gone. It got postponed and is now "in the queue" of bucket list places I plan to go. The time of year would be our winter in the United States as this is summer down under. This is a rough itinerary for a place I have never been and I understand that some of the stops may not be feasible in the time allotted, but I would rather start broad and scale down, so here are some possibilities:

Day 1 - Fly into **Auckland, New Zealand**
Day 2 - Check into hotel in Auckland.
See One Tree Hill vantage point, Check out the revolving restaurant atop the Sky Tower, Colonial Gingerbread house**s**, walk around Queen Street and Parnell and Ponsonby (a leafy inner suburb with a happening vibe) for coffee or other drinks and people watching.

Have dinner in the Britomart District.

<u>Day 3</u> - Walk around Viaduct Harbor and take a racing Yacht NZL40 ride. Go to Waiheke Island (wine tour). Eat dinner at a restaurant on Viaduct Harbor.

<u>Day 4</u> - Take one hour flight to **Wellington**.

Take cable car to botanical gardens, see the painted Victorian houses. Go to Lambton Quay for dinner.

<u>Day 5</u> - Take a three and a half hour scenic Interislander ferry to **Picton** (have lunch in the quaint town). Walk or bike the Queen Charlotte Track or head on a bus or Uber to **Blenheim** and check into hotel and have dinner.

<u>Day 6</u> - Bike ride to wineries in the morning. Take five hour scenic railway on Coastal Pacific Journeys to **Christchurch**.

<u>Day 7</u> - Explore Christchurch on foot, go to Lyttelon Harbor where the rarest dolphin species are found. Go to University of Canterbury Arts Centre for dinner.

<u>Day 8</u> - Explore Christchurch further. Take a three hour 30 min flight to **Sydney**, **Australia** in the evening. Check into hotel.

<u>Day 9</u> - Explore the city- The Rocks (historic area), Sydney Harbor.

<u>Day 10</u> – Blue Mountains – 90 minutes from Sydney. (Featherdale Wildlife Park, Koala Sighting, Leura Village with antique shops). There is a gondola ride and train with open sides to see the views.

<u>Day 11</u>- Explore Sydney - Bohindi beach.

<u>Day 12</u>- Fly to **Melbourne,** check into hotel, and explore Melbourne. Great Ocean road – Twelve Apostles, Tree Top Adventure (Otway Fly Treetop Adventures) for those that enjoy ziplining.

<u>Day 13</u>- Phillip Island - Penguin Parade, Koala Conservation center, Summerland Beach.

Day 14- Rent a car and drive to Healesville – wineries and cider mills and an animal sanctuary with kangaroos, koala bears, and more /Barossa Valley Tanunda (wine town) (45 min from Adelaine).

Day 15 - Kangaroo Island (75 miles from Adelaine) where the sheep outnumber people and there are armies of kangaroos, koalas, wallabies, and fairy penguins.

Day 16 - Tasmania Island – Hobart area and check into hotel.

Day 17 - Explore Tasmania.

Day 18 - Fly back home.

10-Day Argentina Group Tour Itinerary

I took a very similar trip to Argentina with Jeff literally just before Covid hit so we were lucky to squeeze it in before taking a year plus hiatus from traveling (as we all were forced to do). I still enjoy traveling with Jeff alone at times which gives me a chance to explore, document, and plan for where to take future group travelers. This is what I came up with as a possible group trip for this part of the world.

Day 1 - Fly into **Buenos Aires** and get settled into living accommodations.

Accommodations in either Palermo or South Palermo, Ricoletta, San Telmo, or the Art District.

Walk the neighborhood and get familiar with immediate surroundings.

Eat dinner in local restaurant with recommendations.

Day 2 - Grab breakfast locally and get on the On and Off City Bus Tour to get a lay of the land and see the whole city. We actually did this so we know it is worth doing in this particular city. Recommended stops (skipping the one where accommodations are):

Visit the Japanese Tea Garden

Walking tour in <u>La Boca</u> to have a guide show the meaning of the different murals and graffiti (definitely in the morning and not on Sundays, reserve in advance).

Walk around <u>San Telmo</u> and visit the open market – good for lunch and shopping.

Walk around <u>Palermo and South Palermo</u> – good for lunch and shopping.

Walk around the <u>Art District</u> – good for lunch and shopping.

Walk around <u>Ricoletta</u> – good for lunch shopping and visiting the cemetery.

Eat <u>Asado BBQ</u> traditional dinner *with a local* - reservations required in advance. A very personal experience and a way to learn the culture. We did book this when we went and it is where we met the nice couple from Australia that we ended up spending time with on two other occasions while in Buenos Aires. For a group, it would be nice to have the whole place to ourselves in a private home with the host who will cater to our specific group.

<u>Day 3</u> - Visit the areas missed or wanting to revisit from day two or take a half day train ride to small town of <u>Tigre</u>.

Dinner in <u>Puerto Madera</u>, Buenos Aires on the water.

<u>Day 4</u> - Fly to **San Carlos de Bariloche, Patagonia** (Stay in hotel in town near or on the water).

Walk around town – lots of great clothing, chocolate shops, and restaurants in a beautiful setting overlooking the lake. Take a toboggan ride, which we did!

Eat dinner at <u>Alto del Fuego</u> and have a drink in the beer garden adjacent to it.

<u>Day 5</u> - Have a breakfast buffet (reservations required) at the <u>Laio Laio Hotel Resort</u> – and walk around the beautiful all-inclusive property on the lake.

Visit the <u>Tom Wesley Farm and Brewery</u> and take a sunset horse-back ride from there (reservations required).

Eat dinner in town at one of the recommended restaurants.

<u>Day 6</u> - Fly or ferry to **Ushuaia, Patagonia**.

Walk the town and get settled. Dinner at a recommended restaurant.

<u>Day 7</u> - Hike and see the waterfalls.

<u>Day 8</u> - Fly to **Mendoza** and check into <u>Cacheuta Thermal Baths Hotel and Spa</u> – this property is in the Andes Mountains and has a variety of different temperature pools, massage options, and a waterpark with slides and a lazy river.

<u>Day 9</u> - Spend the day at the spa and then drive to <u>Terazzas de Andes Winery</u> where we will stay in the guest house on the property.

Dinner in the nearby quaint town of <u>Chacras de Corio</u> at an outdoor restaurant - Dantesco.

<u>Day 10</u> - Tour and Lunch pairing at <u>Bodega Ruca Malen</u> (five minutes from where we are staying) for a fabulous and leisurely lunch.

A late dinner catered to us at Terazzas de Andes winery.

7-Day Cabo Group Trip Itinerary

Jeff and I regularly go to Cabo. (*It sort of replaced our annual Hawaii trips over the last three years because it's closer and easier to get to especially using the Tijuana border express and flying out of that airport instead of San Diego International*). We also have a friend who lives there, Ricardo, who is in the hospitality and tour business and he takes good care of us. Our last trip there was in April of 2023 and because the weather is perfect at that time of year and we discovered some wonderful new places to stay, visit, and eat (that not everyone even knows about), I put together this group itinerary that I plan to do next year:

Thursday – Arrive at the **San Jose Del Cabo** airport @1:30pm ish. Check into the El Encanto Inn and Suites, a beautiful boutique hotel with gardens, a pool, and restaurant with live music. The location of this hotel is right in the heart of downtown San Jose del Cabo, filled with other great restaurants, wonderful live musicians, and numerous art galleries all in walking distance. We learned about this place a few years ago and are now becoming regulars there. It is great for groups as well.

5:00pm - Meet in the lobby to do the Art Walk (which is every Thursday) together.

7:00pm - Family dinner outside with live music at a nearby restaurant, then explore various bars and musical performances throughout the town.

Friday – Breakfast on your own either at the hotel or many other choices just feet away from our hotel.

10:30am – Get picked up to go to Acre Resort, an oasis only ten minutes away. This hidden resort has a beautiful pool with bar, two restaurants, a bike path, and animal sanctuary with peacocks running wild and enclosures for roosters and their babies, goats, donkeys, horses, and even a camel. Additionally Acre Resorts has a dog rescue program where you can visit and pet the 20-something dogs they have and, should your heart desire, even adopt one to bring home!

They also have other activities such as daily morning yoga at 9:00am, yard games such as bocce ball, ping pong, and pickleball as well as cooking, mixology, and art classes. We will spend two nights enjoying this resort with both leisure time and some planned group activities.

Saturday – Enjoy Acre Resort.

Sunday – 9:00am Choices! You have the following options: Yoga, a bike ride, visiting with the animals, relaxing at the pool where you can read/swim, or sleep in. Complimentary pastry, coffee, and juice between 8:00am-11:00am.

11:00am – Be checked out and ready for pick up to go to <u>Flora Farms</u>, about five minutes away, with a few shops, beautiful grounds, a brewery, and a perfume making experience. We will enjoy the activities and have a nice farm-to-table lunch at their restaurant.

2:30pm- Get picked up to go to **Cabo San Lucas** (about a 30 minute drive) and get checked into hotel near the beach and walking distance to some great restaurants and the marina. Dinner on your own.

Monday – Breakfast/lunch on your own.

1:00pm - Group boat ride to <u>Medano Beach</u> and a few other spots.

Leisure time to rent jet skis, parasail, etc.

8:00pm Group dinner at <u>JM Steakhouse</u> (where I may get the opportunity to entertain you and sing, as I did with the musicians last time we were there).

Tuesday – Breakfast on your own.

11:00am – Get picked up to go to <u>Todos Santos</u>, about an hour drive, where there are nice beaches and a variety of good restaurants. Ricardo, our tour guide, will show us around the beaches and we will have a food tasting day. Get back around 7:00pm and free time to party some more or relax.

Wednesday – 9:30am -Group breakfast.

10:45am – Get picked up for airport.

May 2023 Italy, Greece, and Istanbul, Turkey Trip

This trip was the most recent of trips and came just in time before publishing this book so I decided to include it and write it in a more journal form to give more depth and a colorful explanation. I included not just where we went and what we did, but also how I felt throughout the trip. It can be also looked at as a "research trip" for offering you some insight into these wonderful places as well as my consideration of them for group travel. This particular trip was another combination of a couple's trip and existing group travel trip.

We started off in Rome for a few days before joining Back Stage Pass Travel with Susan and Geoff Tate and a number of friends we met on previous group trips along with some new faces. We probably knew half of the 30 people on this one, but now have double the friends we had before the trip started. That's how it works with group travel.

Things noteworthy of mentioning, starting with our international flight from San Diego to Rome, were that we had two long layovers (making our overall travel door to door time 27 hours). I think this may have been our longest "travel day" ever, with the exception of our journey to Singapore, referenced in an earlier chapter. The nice part about this is now Jeff has a lounge pass so at many airports we get to not only relax in a quieter environment then sitting at crowded gates, but we also get free hot meals and drinks. Sometimes they even have showers when we need some freshening up. I took advantage of this on our second layover in the Frankfurt, Germany airport because that layover alone was over seven hours. It also gave me a chance to continue working on this book, so no time wasted!

Once we finally arrived in **Rome**, we were greeted by our driver (*rather than choosing the train with all of our heavy luggage*). We stayed in a wonderful Airbnb apartment I booked with a very large living room, bedroom, and bathroom fully equipped with a round Roman bathtub and a bidet. We were tired and it was getting late, but luckily there was a fantastic restaurant on the bottom floor of our building where we enjoyed our first Italian dinner on the patio in the Trevi neighborhood.

The next morning we got picked up just outside our apartment by our two drivers for a Vespa Tour of Rome! We contemplated renting them and driving ourselves but after reading reviews and learning particularly from one "motorcycle veteran" that he would not even drive one on the busy Roman streets, I opted not to take that chance. It was more relaxing, but still exhilarating at times, weaving through narrow pedestrian streets. Our drivers were nice and the one whose English was better gave us some history of the sites to which they took us. We were lucky to be spared a partially sunny day with no rain (*this was in May, after all*), since the rest of our Italy stay involved a number of wet days.

After our Vespa thrill ride, we were dropped off at <u>Mister 100 Tiramisu</u> restaurant where they had a long list of types of Tiramisu options. We wanted lunch, not dessert, so we did not get what most came for, but ordered a very nice charcuterie board with meats and cheeses and were satisfied with that.

That afternoon we had a walking tour of the <u>Jewish Ghetto</u> and <u>Travestere</u> areas. The Tiber river and <u>Tiberine Island</u> separated the two and, once a prison, is now a functional hospital. Some other interesting things I remember learning on this tour is that when you see a statue of a soldier on a horse and only one of the four legs is raised, it means that soldier died of natural causes. If the front two legs are raised, it signifies he died in battle.

In the Jewish Ghetto of Rome, even before World War II, Jews were forced to rent rather own a home unless they agreed to convert to Christianity. Even if they didn't, they were forced to attend church. They did not have the same rights as the Roman Catholics or Christians in terms of jobs either, and had to take less desirable ones, again, unless they fully converted. Many were imprisoned or killed for speaking their mind or other minor offenses and even women were killed, which our guide agreed with my assumption that it was probably to prevent procreation. What these families needed to do was disperse so that there were not concentrated amounts of Jews in one area. Unfortunately this meant they had to separate from their family members. Remember, this was even before the Holocaust, which of course, made things even worse.

As we saw in Prague and other European countries, on the side-walks where Jewish families were stripped from their homes with little or no warning and taken to concentration camps, there are metal plated emblems left in their memory. You could read the inscriptions of names, dates of birth, and dates of death (if known) as well as the name of the concentration camp to which they were taken. We saw one of these on our walking tour which had a family of three (youngest member only nine months old), taken to Auschwitz. I studied the dates of the three members. According to my calculations on timing, I determined the adult male was taken there and kept alive for over a year (probably because they put him to work as an able body), the grown woman died in a shorter time, and the infant had either died of malnutrition or was killed only days after being taken the to the camp.

I find it interesting that what we, in the United States, only read about in history books, Europeans can still see remnants of in the historical sites of their own backyards. There are ruins that remain scattered throughout cities and villages all across Europe. Europeans have constant reminders of what happened on their very land either thousands of years ago (*such as the caves in Austria mentioned earlier*) or, in the case of World War II, not even a hundred years ago. Being so far removed, as we are in America, does not give us the same appreciation for this kind of history that you get from traveling to these places; and it changes you.

The last part of our day ended with a special Airbnb Experience dinner at a private home hosted by an Italian family. (*It is such a great way to get into the culture and I described earlier in this chapter where we did a similar thing in Buenos Aires, Argentina, which was just us and one other couple at that time.*) The Rome experience had a total of ten people who were from Canada, the UK, Australia, and the U.S. We shared fun travel stories, talked about our lives at home and what we did for a living, and took a few group pictures at the end. We learned from the host about the culture of being in an Italian family's home and the different foods she had prepared (which were all delicious). It was the best pasta carbonara I ever tasted!

Having at least one dinner this way is such a different and more intimate experience than going to one of many restaurants. I highly recommend looking into these opportunities if you come across them and I usually find them on Airbnb. I also would not hesitate to book at least one group dinner this way in my group travel itinerary.

The following day was another wet day and so we had a short umbrella walk to breakfast nearby at the <u>White Elephant Café</u> in Trevi. On our way there, there were sirens and crowds of people and we were told by our Airbnb host not to worry. It was a visit from President Zelenski (the current President of Ukraine who was to meet with the Italian Prime Minister and Pope John Paul). It was interesting to watch the brigade come through, not once, but a second time later that day as well.

We left this day open to explore other historic sites of Rome but because we did not want to venture too much in the rain or wait in long lines, we chose to stroll through Villa Borghese Park, which was lovely. We then explored the Trevi neighborhood in more depth and found a great restaurant to eat dinner at later.

We felt the need to just rest at our place until we got hungry for the remainder of that day. *Oftentimes, jet lag will set in once the initial excitement dissipates. I believe that when you are in a new place and there is so much to do and see, it's important to take advantage of all that you can't do at home. However, when there is any lull in the action, try to give yourself space from the hustle and bustle of not just your sight-seeing but also a break from your regular life's stressors. Of course, the rain made that choice somewhat easier for us.*

Our Back Stage Pass Tuscany Tour began at noon on the Sunday after we arrived in Rome. With a few days to acclimate to European life and the time difference, it was perfect timing. We arranged for a ride to the airport where we met our group (*or you could also say our "new family members" for the week*). We already knew the band members and a few other folks. It was a three and a half hour ride to our Tuscany Villa from Rome. The drive was scenic and had already started with good spirits. From the start, it felt friendly going into the week with good intentions and excitement.

The Villa was in a beautiful, picturesque setting high on a hill with gorgeous views. As the bus approached, Susan Tate greeted us and, soon after, Geoff Tate came out to say his hellos. The band members that were not on the bus with us were already at the Villa prepping for our arrival. It felt warm and welcoming and Susan had a nice layout of meats, cheeses, and wine as we got settled in and got our room assignments.

It happened to be Mother's Day so I had the idea of taking a picture and video of all the ladies who were also mom's together as a bonding moment. With the exception of one couple, who brought their 27 year old daughter on the trip, no one else had their mothers or children with them for the Mother's Day holiday. It felt like the right thing to do to take some fun and goofy pictures together to break the ice. That first night we had a fabulous dinner, as was true for all the nights that we had home cooked meals at the Villa. I will now go through highlights of the week.

In the week we were in **Tuscany** we had quite a bit of rain but it did not stop us from doing the touristy activities such as a horse drawn carriage ride, walking the narrow, cobblestone streets and alleys in the medieval villages, shopping for souvenirs, taking in the views from hilltops with breathtaking photos, and, of course, trying out some amazing restaurants. We were lucky enough to visit the following places: **Florence, San Gimignano, Sienna, Monteriggioni, and Certaldo**. We were supposed to stop in Montepulciano for lunch on the way back to Rome on our last day but, due to the quick turn-around of our group leaving and the next week long group coming that same day, there was no time to include that. Regardless, it felt like a very full and complete week with all we did.

After each day excursion (with the exception of one night in Siena) we not only came back to a home cooked meal, but also hours of fantastic live music. Other highlights were that I got to talk to Susan about tips for how to run a group travel business and she had some thought provoking questions for me to answer and think about. We have similar ideas about types of excursions and activities to plan. The main difference is that she has her husband, Geoff Tate, the celebrity, which draws people in who want to vacation with him, essentially. What I have to offer, in comparison, is my years of experience with group dynamics and knowing how to engage people in deeper conversation for the purpose of identifying and carrying out goals to improve the self. Although the target audience may differ, we have similar itineraries, with "family dinners" and unique sight-seeing experiences.

Susan understood my purpose and suggested I may want to target people that have never traveled to places like Europe. I agree I could offer that group an enormous amount of information and perhaps comfort. I also think I could interest people that have been to Europe a number of times and saw the main tourist attractions, but are curious about the more rural, less traveled places that are not as infested with tourists. Perhaps I can have a "First Timers" group and a more "Seasoned Traveler" group, where the itineraries would be different. I never feel like my second or third time going to a place is ever like the first time. This is neither good nor bad, it just is. Taking first timers would be exciting to see the looks on their faces as they see amazing sights for the first time. Taking seasoned travelers would be more exploratory and would allow people to share their knowledge with one another as we venture together on our journey. Both would be equally satisfying.

After our fun-filled week in Tuscany, we flew to **Paros**, (not Paris, but a small island in Greece). We stayed at a wonderfully located Airbnb – Lochagoi Georguoi Gravari, Paros, 844 00, Greece. It was advertised with the word "retreat" in it. It was not equipped for a group by any means, but a great little apartment right in the heart of the village of Parikia. It was tucked away in a corner where it was quiet, but still had an adorable and tasty pizza place literally steps away. We actually had our best meal in Parikia at a restaurant called Apollon Garden Restaurant down one of the side alleys and just around the corner from the Pirate Bar, which was a very cozy place for a drink. Jeff got a drink that was lit on fire!

Paros is the perfect balance between not being too touristy and crowded, yet having enough to do and see with three villages to explore. The main villages are: Parikia (where we stayed, where most of the island excursions and ferries port, plenty of restaurants along the water and within the alleys of the village and great shopping with good prices); Nassou (with more hotels and more upscale restaurants and shopping with a little more nightlife than Parikia), and a hilltop village called Lefkos with three or four restaurants, hotels, specialty shops, and art galleries. Note that all of these places can be driven to either by car, motorcycle, or quad within 20-30 minutes.

We loved this island even more than Santorini just because it was not overcrowded. We had no lines to wait in, got a table immediately everywhere we dined, and people were very friendly and happy to chat and share their pride and love for the island.

Plus, it is easy to island hop or fly into Athens or wherever when you need a change of pace. *We have been toying with the idea of taking a year to live in various parts of Europe, and Paros has now become one of the possibilities. Other places I am considering are: Lisbon, Portugal; Sorrento, Italy; Valencia, Spain, and Vienna, Austria.*

Another highlight in Paros was carving a token to bring home out of a slab of marble at a Marble Workshop. I had never used power tools before and John Batista (*our teacher from France who ran the workshop*) showed me step by step how to safely create a design, carve, and polish a piece of marble slab into whatever shape I desired. Jb's Atelier – Marble Workshop, Kampos 844 00, Greece (*200 m from the kite surf beaches*) was the place we got to create our pieces, overlooking the sunset.

The shop was not luxurious but John was friendly, helpful, encouraging, and generous with his time. We were the only people in the workshop so we got individual attention. Jeff made a marble heart which came out pretty well. I was undecided and ended up making a diamond instead of a heart because the straight edges were much easier to cut. I also wanted it to be functional so I made a deep hole so that it could house jewelry, nuts or whatever can fit. It also rocks back and forth because it was curved on the bottom versus flat. Jeff said that every day he sees it, as I had been using it to put my jewelry in at night on this trip, it looks better to him (*whatever that means*). I am glad it is growing on him.

Our next Greek island was **Milos**. We took a night ferry there which was only two hours with a quick stop at a small island along the way. Our accommodations were Hotel En Milo, Pollonia, Milos 84800, Greece. I highly recommend this hotel because it was in a very quiet and peaceful town. It had about eight restaurants and a few coffee and specialty shops. Our specific hotel had a nice pool across the street from a swimmable beach that you could easily get to without having to climb down a cliff. However the more challenging swimming hole options that we saw from afar were breathtaking and plenty of people looked like they were making a day out swimming in the pristine oceans below.

Another other nice thing about Hotel En Milo was that you got a nice full breakfast spread each morning and got to choose between the American or Greek breakfast or combine what you liked from each. We chose the option of getting it served to our veranda off our room overlooking the ocean. It was delightful. The staff was super hospitable.

Milos did offer a number of beautiful beaches in which to swim including the one in Pollonia, but mainly the bigger town of <u>Adamas</u> (where the commuter ferries port). Adamas had plenty of water activities and island hopping day excursions, but Pollinia also had some. Having a quiet place like Pollonia to land each night may be nice if you just want relaxation. Adamas was more populated with more restaurants and shops, but it seems to me that if you are going to Milos, you probably are looking for a small town vibe. Pollonia and The En Milo hotel could easily be one of many group trip destinations for a Greek island hopping adventure.

We explored the island on a quad and Jeff was fine with me being the driver for the entire day. It was very fun and we feel we got to know the whole island. We visited the catacombs, which if taking a group, I would definitely set up a group tour to actually be able to explore deep within the caves. We visited the ruins of an old theater and saw the Venus de Milo statue.

We also happened across an unusual looking place that looked like a sign for a hotel in a cave but it was on top a steep hill. We took the quad up and enjoyed the view but it looked like nothing else was there, then realized there was a hotel hidden in a crevice of the mountain. We were curious and followed a couple walking in towards their room and this UK couple was nice enough to show the inside. It was amazing not just because of the view but each of the six rooms had its own private small swimming pool on the balcony. It also had a common area where you could easily hold a gathering for cocktails. Exciting possibilities!

Next we flew to **Athens** and checked into the <u>Acropolis View Hotel</u>, 10 Webster Str. & Robertou Galli, Athens, Attica, 117 42, Greece. I recommended this hotel for its location near the Acropolis and easy walking distance to the area of <u>Plaka</u> and the surrounding areas. It has endless neighborhoods full of restaurants and streets lined with shops and flea markets, such as <u>Monastiraki</u>. The <u>Thissio</u> area is also a nice choice with more hotel options, not as close to Plaka, but closer to Monastiraki.

We found the people to be very welcoming in Athens as well as all the places we visited in Greece. One funny story about another couple from the UK, who were sitting next to us at dinner our first night in Athens. I was excited to share that our room had a balcony overlooking the Acropolis and the woman said, "I hate to burst your bubble, but just about everywhere you go outside in the surrounding areas, you have a view of the Acropolis". As we found this to be true, I didn't feel our room with a balcony view was so special.

In fact the hotel name itself, "Acropolis View Hotel" is accurate and not misleading, it's just that it is not "special" for that area. As the receptionist explained the next day, "if you ever get lost, just look for the Acropolis as your landmark and you will know where you are because you can see it from everywhere". We actually did take his advice and used it as our compass (or GPS) if you will. Interestingly, there are no skyscrapers in Athens, and that's because of the simple fact that no building is allowed to be taller than the Acropolis, which would be difficult to achieve but nevertheless. "Acro" stands for extreme and "polis" is city. This extreme city is not only extreme in its height, but also extreme in that it has thousands of years of rich history. My point is that Athens, as a whole, is built around and in consideration of The Acropolis, and actually that, in and of itself, is pretty special.

For our last night in Athens, we did venture away from the popular touristy area to a neighborhood called Koukaki, where the same hotel receptionist told me that that is where the locals go to eat and hangout. It was ten minute walk from our hotel and it was bustling with locals laughing, drinking, and socializing. It was a very different feel than the Plaka area; more casual, not as pretty, but lively, and still safe. Our dinner was okay, not our best meal, but we were glad to have experienced another side of Athens.

After dinner, we walked ten minutes back to the Plaka area and we approached a restaurant where we were solicited the night before by a very friendly waiter. He actually remembered us and said, "I was looking for you, where did you go?" He smiled and offered us a nice seat perfect for people watching as we apologized for already having ate dinner elsewhere. The waiter was just as happy to seat us simply for a drink, and was in line with the hospitality trend I observed throughout our entire Greek experience, as he still pulled out the white table cloth for us.

Immediately after sitting, a gregarious man with his wife and another couple at the neighboring table befriended us, and we all were in deep conversation within minutes. They were from the states as well – Georgia and Ohio. Their story is what I found interesting and fits into why I love to travel, so I thought to include it. The couples met each other thirteen years ago in a bar in New York while traveling. They hit it off immediately and have been best friends ever since and now travel together twice a year. After an hour of conversation and seeing that our love for traveling was a common thread, we actually exchanged information with them and it is possible they may come on my Croatia trip (or perhaps a different one in the future). You just never know who you are going to meet when traveling and making these random connections with people can be life-changing, and it just takes one conversation to start it.

I have so much to say about our next destination, Istanbul, Turkey, and unlike any other place we have been, I had some trepidation before traveling there. However, once acclimated, it was definitely much more comfortable and wonderful than I had imagined.

So, let me now backtrack a little.

Our taxi driver in Athens on the way to the airport the next morning had a plethora of information about our next destination, **Istanbul,**

Turkey, and his perspective was not as enthusiastic as we wanted it to be. The consensus of those with whom I spoke, in addition to the taxi driver, say the food is fabulous and there are a variety of places to see with changes in scenery from each neighborhood in terms of the culture and people of different backgrounds and beliefs. This also could be a negative however in that there is sometimes tension, dishonesty, and violence. The taxi driver admitted to us that he did have a bad situation occur last time he was in Istanbul well over 25 years ago and would not take his family there anytime soon. Jeff also knows a Greek guy who said he would not go to Istanbul at this time. Many others have warned us that people in Istanbul (of course not everybody but enough to earn the reputation) are aggressive. The taxi driver also warned us not to take a random taxi when in Istanbul because they not only will tell you one price and then double it once you are in the car, but he also said they carry guns and could demand you give them money, possessions, and who knows what else. This got me nervous.

In America we are not used to being in those situations with any level of frequency and Jeff and I certainly did not want to expose ourselves to it even one time, so we took measures to avoid it. While in that cab ride to the airport, we secured a taxi driver ahead of time through a legitimate company which had high ratings on TripAdvisor. Luckily, it worked out even better than we expected. We liked this driver's professionalism and promptness so much that we secured him for our ride back to the airport after our four day stay.

Other things we were warned about were pick-pocketers and were told not to walk around like a tourist with our phones out and maps in our hands because we would be a clear target (*I made sure Jeff fully understood this*). So, unlike other areas of Europe, we were forewarned that it just may not be as safe. When I asked the Greek taxi driver if they like Americans, he said not really and that they don't like Greeks either because there are years of battle for land that has gone back and forth in history. He explained that Istanbul was formally owned by Greece but the Turks conquered it in 1922 and renamed it from Constantinople to Istanbul, so there is some bitterness there. I gathered, from his last explanation, that if you are Greek in particular, you may feel somewhat more threatened here than someone of a different origin.

Fortunately I deduced correctly, as in our experience as Americans, once the few days of culture shock faded, we actually felt safer than some areas in the U.S. We even went against what the Greek taxi driver advised and took a taxi off the street at night just to get back to our hotel quicker than taking the subway, bus, or metro (*which we had also learned very well in our four day stay*). The Turkish taxi driver was very kind and, in fact, had some of his own concerns for us. He told us to be careful around <u>Taksim Square</u> where he dropped us off because there was some chaos and celebratory behaviors with fireworks after a football (*soccer to us*) championship game that just took place that day. He was accurate in that it was chaotic but no violence erupted as he had predicted.

Taksim Square does seem like the place where all hell would break loose as it is a major gathering place and always very crowded, so keep that in mind future Turkish travelers. On the other hand, it is the place where the soul of the city lives and it is lively and full of visual stimuli everywhere you look. One of our favorite meals on this whole trip was in that area called <u>Meat Moot</u>, where you get a huge slab of either beef or lamb for the table with a variety of dipping sauces. Our hotel was a few blocks between Taksim and Chihangir neighborhoods.

I loved the one four corner area in <u>Chihangir</u> where there were coffee shops facing one another and people just chilled outside for hours socializing or just taking in the day and people watching. The neighborhood is one which has narrow, winding streets, scattered restaurants, and wine bars as well. Our last afternoon in Istanbul (a three week trip in total) was spent reminiscing there.

Another thing we were told in order to prep for Turkey was to dress more conservatively, especially women. No shorts, sleeveless or tight-fitting clothing (and in mosques women need to wear a scarf of something covering their head), so I was prepared. However, once in Istanbul I observed that it really depends on what part of the city or outskirts you are in. For the majority of places that tourists frequent, especially the mosques, woman do need to dress without showing skin and need to cover their head. Other areas like the museums, the head need not be covered. If you go to more modern areas on the outskirts such as <u>Nissantasi</u> (an upscale shopping area with nice restaurants), pretty much anything goes for women.

I noticed a woman with full head to toe black clothing and a Punjab sitting in a restaurant sadly stirring some rice around her plate without taking off her face covering. Next to her was her husband enjoying his full loaded plate of food. That didn't seem right to me, and I didn't stay long enough to satisfy my curiosity about how or if she would actually eat. Other than that incident, I would say most people I witnessed (men and women) seemed to be high-spirited in Istanbul.

Our first night staying in Istanbul was a Saturday night, and to our surprise, directly across the street from our hotel was a techno night club that is open from 10:00pm until about 8:00am. We saw people standing in line to get in before we went to bed and there was not much noise, but then suddenly after 2:00am all the way until about 5:30pm it was super loud with music and people socializing and enjoying themselves. Apparently the other bars close at 2:00am and then the real "fun" began on our street (little did we know).

In addition to our first night being a Saturday "party" night, the next day, Sunday, the presidential election happened to be going on. It was a sight to see all the people who were happy with the result honking their horns and riding on hoods of cars and in trunks waving flags. It was comparable to when Trump won the election. The only difference is there were no protests from the opposing side. Many were not happy that this president who they say is a dictator/authoritarian and does not promote any advancement of women's rights, remained and is continuing to be president after 23 years. At least in the U.S. it caps off at eight. Needless to say, it was the second night of not much sleep due to caravans of cars honking as they passed by our street well into the wee hours. Not complaining, just reporting the unique experience.

Another memorable observation that I have of Turkey are the hundreds of cats everywhere and random cat homes and bowls of food and water scattered around. These cats roam the streets, wait outside of restaurants, and find comfy places to sleep like in flower pots or on top of scooters. There are also dogs that were laying in the middle of sidewalks with people having to navigate, but willingly did, around them. The dogs did not seem phased by the chaos of the city in the slightest. They were not on leashes, and had chips in their ears.

One time while waiting for a green light (*and mind you, jaywalking is actually very common everywhere we went*), it was quite amusing that the dogs knew that waiting for the green light was the safest option. Again, not on a leash, just one of the citizens in the crowd. It was actually rare to see dogs who were owned by one owner or family. In the time we were there, I can count on one hand the number of dogs on leashes. There were no dog fights, barking, or aggression of any kind. Just calm, cool, and collected animal species roaming the streets like they owned the place, which was actually true in the sense that they received just as much respect, if not more, than their human counterparts.

When we were waiting at a metro stop and there were about twelve people standing waiting for the next metro, nobody would dare disrupt the three cats sprawled out on the only bench. I don't see that being the case in the U.S. for some reason, either humans would shove the animal aside to sit, or the animal would never assume they even had the right to take the seat of a human being. Even the animal culture was different in Turkey and I found it fascinating. A local revealed that people do not tend to own pets as they do in the states, but rather the government funds their care and that is why they are so well taken care of and so well behaved. It was such a beautiful and refreshing thing to see and made me smile every day that I got to enjoy their presence.

Istanbul, interestingly, is partially in Europe and partially in Asia. We stayed in the Europe side in the areas I described above. Still on the Europe side, we also enjoyed the Galata area where there were ferries coming in and out of the dock constantly and four story restaurants lined along the water with people fishing directly above them off a bridge. In addition to great people watching, you also occasionally see a fish being pulled up on a hook from the bridge above wherever you are seated as you enjoy your meal. Orokoy, if you have more than a few days in Istanbul, is an easy jaunt on the bus and is quieter, less touristy, and has a handful of great restaurants right on the water near the ferry port.

If you have never had a Turkish breakfast, be hungry and try one if you make it to this part of the world; such a variety of cheeses, meats, and dips for your bread. The different small plates and bowls literally took up the whole table and was a great way to start the day. The Sultanahmet district had many of the historical sites like the Blue Mosque, Hague Sophia, and Basilica and is a great option to find an accommodation for its quieter, safe, and beautiful village-like location. Although we did not stay there, our friends who were in Istanbul just a week prior to our visit recommended staying at The Henna Hotel which is in that area and when we went to check it out, I can easily see why. This hotel had a beautiful rooftop with panoramic views of the city and mosques. The area is also not too far from the Grand Bazaar and the Egyptian Spice Bazaar, where you can find just about anything you need shopping-wise.

Speaking of shopping, it is quite an experience when it comes to shopping in Istanbul for things like leather coats or Turkish carpets. Turks really know how to sell their goods! "Once you accept the tea, it's over!" as one of our friends who had been to Turkey commented.

It is very true. You become almost like family in a sense that they invite you into their comfortable living space and you engage in lengthy conversation and the beginnings of a friendship and, once you feel special (and they have a way of succeeding at this), then the negotiations begin.

It was actually a pleasant experience for us because in the leather coat experience, we ended up purchasing three nice quality coats made of premium leather for a fraction of what we would pay in the States. In the Turkish carpet experience, we had an in-depth and lengthy conversation with an educated and well-spoken (English speaking) gentleman who had lived in the states for many years. Although he had gorgeous carpets and educated us about the difference between carpets and rugs, he was okay with the fact that we really were not in the market for one and we left with his friendly comment, "We're still friends". He even continued our conversation for a while after he knew no sale was taking place without mentioning the carpets again that he had laid out in front of our feet. I appreciated his sincerity as well as the "no pressure".

Other areas I would recommend staying, unless you don't want to be that far from other sites, are in the Asian side, specifically the <u>Moda</u> area. It is furnished with restaurants and endless shops and flea market type vendors where you can bargain for good deals. We wanted to check out the Barts Manco Museum which exhibits Turkish 70's and 80's rock in the Moda area but, due to the election, it was closed. We also really liked the <u>Bagdat Caddesi</u> area with a Bohemian culture and affordable restaurants and shops. In walking distance to that area, we found beautiful upscale apartment homes with nice restaurants on the first floor of many, and it was also blocks from a nice walking path along the water. It reminded us a lot of San Diego and parts of it almost looked identical. We sort of felt right at home there!

Overall, after my initial culture shock and nervousness about being in a country where you have to worry about your safety more than I am accustomed to, I felt pretty comfortable and found Istanbul very inviting, helpful, and accommodating. It is a very beautiful place, especially when the mosques are all lit up at night. Every so often all other music is shut down that may be playing in the restaurants and all you can hear is the chanting from the nearby mosques echoing in the streets.

I think Istanbul would be a good choice in taking a group in particular because it is one of those places that people may feel more at ease doing with a group and with people they trust. I have made some connections while there for transportation and contact information for people that speak English who know the history well so that one is now in the queue.

8-Day 2024 Croatia Group Trip Itinerary!

I already have people signed up for this one and it will be my first overseas international Life Your Life Travel trip that will be launching in June of 2024! Here is the proposed itinerary and exact content in the flyer that went out to my registered travelers:

Day 1- You will have free transportation to our first stay in Trogir (a charming old village) at a boutique hotel with a welcome drink upon your arrival! Once you settle in, you can explore the village and we will all join for a welcome dinner.

Day 2 – Enjoy breakfast in Trogir and depart to Krka National Park and Waterfalls. By evening we will arrive at our next destination – one of my favorite places, Zadar. We will spend two nights at a boutique hotel in the center of historic old town. You can explore the area filled with shops and many eateries off cobblestone streets as well as overlooking the ocean and have some free time to enjoy a restaurant of your choice.

Day 3 – We will explore the wonders of Zadar such as the Sun Salutations and The Sea Organ and then drive to the island of Pag (the moonlike island) where lace-making, cheese tasting from sheep's milk, and salt mines can be explored. If times allows, we will take a short ferry ride to <u>Ugljan</u> (the olive island). Dinner on your own either on Ugligan or in Zadar.

<u>Day 4</u> – We will drive to <u>Split</u> and do some sightseeing at our leisure and check into our hotel right in the heart of the old town area near the water. We will join for a group dinner at a local restaurant.

<u>Day 5</u> – Early morning ferry for a speed boat excursion to the <u>Blue Cave</u> and <u>Hvar</u> where we will get to swim at the pebble beach, walk the cobblestone streets, look for dolphins, and visit a farm with donkeys and chickens as well as enjoy traditional Dalmatian cuisine.

<u>Day 6</u> – Take a morning ferry from Split towards <u>Dubrovnik</u> with a stop on the beautiful island of <u>Miljet</u>. We will then continue on to Dubrovnik where we will check into our hotel just outside the walled city by the water. There will be plenty of dinner options to choose from and you are free to make your own plans or eat with fellow travelers.

<u>Day 7</u> – Explore Dubrovnik – free time on your own - options are taking the cable car to the top of <u>Mt. Srd</u> where there is hiking and a museum and amazing views and/or visit the interesting and beautiful island of <u>Kokrum</u> (only a fifteen minute ferry ride) where you can swim, hike, and see numerous peacocks running wild. Towards early evening we will all meet to walk the top tier perimeter of the walled city with stops along the way to the different bars which overlook the city. We will end the evening with a nice dinner in the heart of the old town together.

<u>Day 8</u> – A half-day red wine tasting excursion in the Pelijesac region where they claim to have some of the best wines in the world – Plavac Mali varietal. We will visit another medieval village, <u>Ston,</u> with one of the longest stone walls in Croatia and also known for the best oysters in the region. Following this excursion, we will have a special last dinner together.

<u>Day 9</u> – The sad day comes when our journey together comes to an end- until next time!

I like to plan just enough to have a great fun-filled, organized experience but yet leave some leeway to have free time (as well as some alone time which is also important during group travel). This allows both flexibility and exploration of things people may not have been aware of prior to the trip, which usually happens and is all part of the excitement.

Other Ideas for Group Travel

Other ideas I have for group travel that were not mentioned in any previous itineraries above include **Portugal**, which I like because is not bombarded by tourism as much as some other places. I had the opportunity to visit Portugal once but I would love to see more of it and take a group there. <u>Lisbon</u> has a Golden Gate Bridge that looks exactly like the one in San Francisco. I looked out of our Airbnb window the morning after we arrived late the night before and I thought I was hallucinating because I had no idea until that moment. I grew up in San Francisco so I was very confused about where I was for a few seconds. It is also hilly in Lisbon, as is SF, so I guess I felt sort of at home with the familiarity of that environment. There is a lot to do and see there and it has a nice blend of old and new.

Another country I love is **Spain** in which I have traveled all over on two separate occasions. Although I love <u>Barcelona</u> (and who doesn't??!), my favorite places in Spain were <u>Granada</u> for the beautiful hilly paths and corridors overlooking the river running through it and <u>Valencia</u>. In Europe I look for cities that have a lot to offer in terms of opportunities for growth, good weather most of the year, efficient transportation, and a combination of historic and medieval flavor mixed with modern conveniences and technology. Valencia has all of that as well as some great beaches. It also is less crowded with tourists than in areas such as Barcelona.

Thailand is a place I went with Jeff early on in our relationship and it was the first international trip I took since childhood, so it was incredibly exciting for me on many levels. I would love to take a group to <u>Phuket</u> (*not pronounced "Fuck It"*) and <u>Phi Phi</u> (actually *is* pronounced "Pee Pee") island, where you are greeted off a two hour boat trek with a delicious cocktail drink and for those of you that used to watch "Fantasy Island", it's exactly like that!

We went to an all-inclusive resort where women went topless in the pools and there were a number of restaurants to choose from each night depending on your mood. The accommodations were huts on stilts above the water. It was romantic and delightful and I could only imagine the fun a group would have in that environment. It would be a perfect retreat location.

<u>Bangkok</u> is a great city with lots to do and would be the place to fly into to spend a few sightseeing days, but then taking a group off the beaten path would be my plan. For example, we went to Satuk, a small village near <u>Buriram</u> were locals live. There was an elephant sanctuary not too far from there that was very interesting and would be a treat to take a group to, however we would not get there as many locals do – families of six or seven piled on a tiny motor scooter built for one to two people (no joke, it was unbelievable to see what people do there).

Africa and Morocco are two other places I have never been nor have researched enough to plan an itinerary yet, but would love to explore either on my own with Jeff or as a group (or perhaps a combo of both). I originally shied away from the latter when I learned they use their left, (or was it right), hand to wipe themselves after doing their business. I am not sure about my comfort level with that, but as long as I do not have to shake hands, I guess hand sanitizer every few minutes can suffice.

All joking aside, I have heard wonderful and interesting things about the place like a section where all the buildings are igloo-like and have a blue tint to them. I have also eaten in Moroccan restaurants and always liked the tangine spice on their meat dishes. African safaris and sleeping in tents in the wild (with a trained guide you trust of course) sounds like a real adventure to experience with a group and everyone I have talked with that has done so raves about it as one of their most memorable trips.

I would also like to venture into **Dubai** (*of course bring your biggest wallet, I know*). It seems to be wealthy and intensely ahead of the times for modern technology with an unbelievable realm of possible activities. I may need to explore this individually before taking a group for obvious reasons.

The list goes on and on and never seems to stop. With each adventure, more ideas are generated for sharing these unique experiences with others. I am always in awe of the abundance of places to go, such that it is near impossible to see it all in one lifetime.

SECTION V

PHOTO GALLERY

Now I can bring some memories to life
sharing pictures taken from some of
the places I described.

Tulum, Mexico

"I will forever have
memories of how moved I
was at the yoga retreat I
attended here."

Argentina

"What makes this country extra special, in addition to the wonderful food and beautiful scenery, is the lively and rich culture. The people are warm and friendly and have a real zest for life and a strong sense of community."

Barcelona, Spain

"From the lively beaches and exciting nightlife to the most detailed architectural buildings, Barcelona is a fascinating, liberal, and culturally diverse city."

Rotterdam, Netherlands

"A very entertaining city with a surprisingly modern and progressive flair."

Vienna, Austria

"This is one of my favorite European
cities. Not only are the intricately
designed churches impressive inside
and out, but the many parks and
entertainment along the Danube river
made it a place I wish to return."

Plitvice Lakes, Croatia

"It literally brought tears to my eyes the first time I was here. I was overwhelmed with its mesmerizing beauty."

Greece

"Nobody can deny the striking
scenery of the Greek islands, but
the warm hospitality of the people
is what makes Greece one of the
most beautiful places in the world."

Rome, Italy

Rome has an incredible mix of modern conveniences, such as the underground metro system, and ancient structures, fountains, and statues. There is something for everybody with its interesting neighborhoods, beautiful parks, and museums.

"Sorrento has a great small town feel with restaurants and bars lined up along the water for a perfect balance of relaxation and fun."

Sorrento and Capri, Italy

"Easily accessible from Sorrento is a 20-minute ferry ride to Capri, which has one of the most stunning views of the Amalfi coast and exciting water excursions such as the Blue Grotto."

France

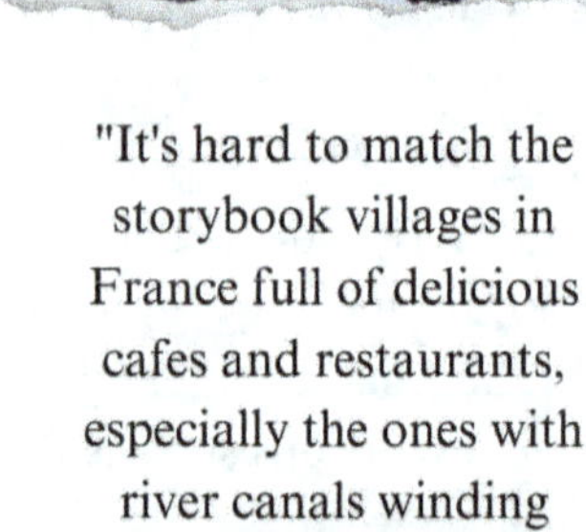

"It's hard to match the storybook villages in France full of delicious cafes and restaurants, especially the ones with river canals winding through."

French Castles

"To see them and tour them is one thing. To live in them for a week long retreat with future lifelong friends is truly magical."

INFORMATION ABOUT SIGNING UP FOR LYLT GROUPS

If you are interested in using my services either to plan an individual trip itinerary, a family reunion, a group trip with friends, or join in as a solo traveler or as a couple on a LYLT trip, please contact me via email. For group travel interest, I will add you to my bimonthly newsletters which will keep you updated on future trips with registration opportunities and other articles and shared experiences of spectacular places we may travel together:

Email: **Drstacy@drstacykimj.com**

Website: **www://Drstacykimj.com**

INDEX

Other Recommended Travel Groups

Other Healers

PERSONAL ACKNOWLEDGEMENT

In terms of those closest to me, I would like to first thank my love and partner in life, Jeff, for being such a great travel companion, trusting me to create our numerous travel itineraries, and for being my inspiration to travel way before retirement. I would like to thank my daughter, Rachel, whom inspired and motivated me to write this book and pursue my dream of starting a group travel retreat business. My son, Josh, who has always been so curious, open, and interested in hearing my ideas about the world and has given me wonderful and honest feedback about this book. I would not be the person I am without all of you by my side.

I would also like to thank all the world travelers and group travel leaders that agreed to be interviewed (whose names are mentioned in Chapter 3). Your insights were so valuable in making salient the meaning that travel has in people's lives.

A special thank you to Saurabh Gupta, Ph.D., who has always been a tremendous supporter of my retreat planning and group travel trips and has nominated me for various positions and related events. This has built my confidence in moving forward in the ways I have.

My friend and book writing soulmate, Lisa Wilson, who was paired with me through an online book writing program and has been with me along this journey also deserves acknowledgement. We have been supporting each other in both our book-writing efforts. It made the process much more enjoyable and motivating to share each phase together and I feel lucky to have gained a new friend with this common interest.

I am very thankful for my old friend Michelle Melotti-Merdon whom I met in my mid 20's while we both were in graduate school in Philadelphia. After over 25 years of losing touch with one another, we reunited and she jumped right back into my life by signing up for a group travel trip I planned for Croatia and was a great support in my writing this book.

I need to give a special thank you to Jesse Gilmore, my daughter Rachel's partner, who has not just been a blessing to our family for being a wonderful human, but has shown eagerness to help not just in this book project but also future travel trips with his photography/videography expertise. I recommend him highly. His website is jshootsraw.smugmug.com and he can be reached via email at jshootsraw@gmail.com.

I appreciate my friends and family very much and feel blessed to have so much love and support on this venture. I look forward to sharing and creating many more life-changing experiences in the years ahead and it is my hope that, when my time has come, others will carry out and follow the beautiful path I am laying out.

ABOUT THE AUTHOR

Dr. Stacy Kim Johnston currently resides in San Diego, California. She received her doctorate from Temple University in Philadelphia in 1998. She continues to work with clients via telehealth with a caseload of 40-50 clients per week, while also pursuing worldwide travel. Dr. Johnston is a singer/songwriter and has a collection of recorded original songs about people and things that have inspired her. She occasionally performs at private events, and sometimes publicly. Her passion for writing, singing, traveling, and healing people through her psychological services and bonding experiences is what gives her life meaning.

If you are interested in listening to her music, you can find her on Spotify under Stacy Kim.